SINO – PAK NEXUS AND

IMPLICATIONS FOR INDIA

SINO – PAK NEXUS
AND
IMPLICATIONS FOR INDIA

By

Colonel MD Upadhyay

Centre for Joint Warfare Studies (CENJOWS)
New Delhi

Vij Books India Pvt Ltd

New Delhi (India)

Published by

Vij Books India Pvt Ltd

(Publishers, Distributors & Importers)
2/19, Ansari Road, Darya Ganj
New Delhi - 110002
Phones: 91-11-43596460, 91-11- 47340674
Fax: 91-11-47340674
e-mail : vijbooks@rediffmail.com
web: www.vijbooks.com

ISBN : 978-93-84464-72-1

The views expressed in the book are of the author and not necessarily those of the Centre for Joint Warfare Studies/publishers.

Contents

1 | BACKGROUND TO SINO – PAK COLLABORATION

Sino – Pak relations were in a dormant state in 1947 at the time of creation of Pakistan. Pakistan was the third non-communist country and first Muslim country to recognize People's Republic of China on 4 January, 1950, after breaking its relations with the Republic of China (Taiwan). The initiation of formal relations between the two countries can be traced back to May 1951, when Pakistan established diplomatic relations with China. Bilateral relations were further strengthened at the Bandung Conference in 1955, when talks between the two heads of state played an important role in promoting, understanding and paving way for friendly relations and mutual assistance between the two countries. In 1961, Pakistan furthered its relations with China when it voted in favour of China's restoration rights in the UN. Military aid from China to Pakistan began in 1966, strategic alliance was formed in 1972 and economic co-operation began in 1979. Maintaining close relations with China has been a central part of Pakistan's foreign policy. The foundation of relations between China and Pakistan took place at the behest of USA during the Cold War period. The U.S. policy at that time was to support any regime which was opposed to Soviet Union and its form of communism. At the outset, Sino-Pak relationship was based on their common security concerns. During the early stages of their relations, both the countries had to face security challenges for their survival. In 1948, Pakistan was engaged in a war against India over Kashmir and in 1950 China was drawn into the Korean War. The Soviet-Chinese union provided strength to China, but there was no international support for China. Meanwhile, Pakistan had joined the U.S. as an ally against the expansion of communism by joining Southeast Asia Treaty Organization (SEATO) in 1954 and the Baghdad Pact in 1955. Although this alliance provided Pakistan with economic and military aid, it was virtually abandoned in its hour of crisis during the 1965 Indo-Pak war. Similarly, during the Sino-Indian conflict in 1962, India received economic and military aid from both USA and USSR. Since both China and Pakistan had fought wars with India, they had a common threat in the neighbourhood which became a strong binding factor for them. When the USSR supported India against China during the Sino-Indian border clash in 1962, Beijing realized that it should normalize relations with the USA. Pakistan played a key role in bringing United States and China to the discussion table and bridged their differences by identifying the Soviet Union as their common enemy. The 1971 Indo-USSR Treaty of Friendship posed another challenge to both Pakistan and China.

Geographical realities also brought both countries together. During the 1950s and 1960s both were considered as weak states. Geographically, both were in near proximity to their rivals. China, which harboured a historical hostility toward Japan and fell off with both India and the Soviet Union during those two decades, has adjoining borders with all three countries. Pakistan on the other hand had unfriendly neighbours-India and Afghanistan-to both its east and its west, a fact that figured prominently in Pakistan's security perspectives. Though geographical proximity and security issues led the two states to come together and without doubt United States played a key role in cementing the Sino-Pak relationship. Pakistan was driven by its paranoia about India, which brought it closer to China. In the early 1960s, Beijing was determined to obtain a hedge in South Asia against what it perceived as India's ambitions. Islamabad's support in the Sino-Indian boundary dispute endorsed China's outreach to its neighbours and China's anti-India policy provided the foundation for the Sino-Pakistani relationship to move forward.

The relationship gathered momentum in 1962, when China and India were engaged in a war over the disputed territory of Aksai Chin and the territory then known as the North East Frontier Agency.

China defeated India. As a last-ditch effort, India approached USA for military support which saw it as an opportunity to gain a foothold in the region against the spread of Soviet and Chinese communism and began providing military support to India. America's other partner in the region, Pakistan, did not look favourably on Washington's support to its enemy. Pakistan had joined the SEATO as well as CENTO in 1954 as part of USA's efforts to establish a barrier around Soviet and Chinese communist powers. Pakistan even gave USA use of a top-secret air base to fly U2 reconnaissance missions over the Soviet Union. In return, the U.S. equipped and trained Pakistan military, which used the equipment and training to strengthen its negotiating position with India in talks over Kashmir and to prepare for a conventional war with India. Therefore for Pakistan, America's support to India in the Sino-Indian conflict was treated as a betrayal.

China took advantage of this rift to reach out to Pakistan. In the early 1960s, both the countries signed two landmark agreements and began joint construction of a major roadway, which added significant weight to their relationship. The first agreement was a bilateral trade pact signed in 1963. The second was the 1963 Sino-Pakistan Frontier Agreement, wherein China ceded more than 1,942 square kilometers to Pakistan and Pakistan on its part recognized Chinese sovereignty over 5,180 square kilometers of area in Northern Kashmir and Ladakh region. The two countries also began collaboration on a major project to build the Trans-Karakoram highway, often referred to as the Friendship Highway. This highway connects the northern areas of Pakistan to the Xinjiang province in China and its construction commenced in 1966 and is considered vital for commercial and strategic purposes.

The security dimension of the relations between the two countries surfaced and became evident during the 1965, Indo-Pak war. China was vocal in its support of Pakistan and deemed India as the aggressor. It even alerted its troops on the Indo-Tibet border to pressurize India. As a result of this, India came under pressure and acted cautiously in order to not displease the Chinese. Considering that 1965 war ended in a stalemate, one can assume that China was instrumental in boosting the morale of Pakistan during the war. Despite that there were no significant gains but every move fortified the friendship and gave Pakistan a sense of security it had always longed for. The Chinese support hailed by the Pakistanis further strengthened friendship.

The Indo – Pak war of 1971 was another occasion for China to offer immense political and diplomatic support for Islamabad. Throughout the Bangladesh crisis, Chinese press and diplomats unleashed a barrage of criticism on India. The escalation of political and diplomatic support for Pakistan was evident throughout the 1971 War. Beijing's assistance to Islamabad was kept up by a constant supply of material, verbal and moral support throughout the crisis. Some movement of Chinese troops was reported, however it did not restrict Indian military actions in East Pakistan. The move was designed to pressurize India psychologically akin to Chinese actions and possible impact during the 1965 War and earn goodwill of Pakistan. However, Pakistan's expectations of a direct Chinese involvement in East Pakistan did not materialize. Despite this, Sino-Pakistan relations did not get negatively affected and China's support was hailed by the Pakistani masses.

During the Soviet invasion of Afghanistan, it was perceived by the Chinese that it was an attempt by the Soviets to expand into South Asia. China feared that if the Soviets were able to gain control of routes to the Indian Ocean, its own lack of an early warning system and sufficient naval forces would not be able to match up with Soviet naval supremacy, and therefore China would be at the Soviet mercy from all sides. China further assumed that Moscow's new found control over Afghanistan would enable the Soviets to locate nuclear weapons just outside the Xinjiang province along the border that was shared by China and Afghanistan. China perceived that a direct military response in Afghanistan would provoke the Soviet forces along its northern border. Meanwhile, Pakistan was also in crisis. It felt that the Soviets would next march into Pakistan which was also believed by China. The mutual concern about the Soviets led China to start providing strategic and military support to the Afghan fighters already being funded and trained by Pakistan to avoid a direct military engagement with superior Soviet forces. Chinese also gave a guarantee to Pakistan that if the Soviets invaded it, China would come to its defence. This period also saw a high rate of exchanges in the top civil and military level for consultations to gain an understanding of each other's stance on bilateral relations and global affairs. An agreement was signed for opening of Khunjerab Pass on the China-Pakistan border which facilitated opening an important transportation link between both the countries. The strengthening of Sino-Pak relations in warding off the Soviets threat signified another important Chinese motivation for befriending Pakistan as it served as a gateway for establishing relations with the Muslim world, as well as provide a route to the South West Asia, Central Asia and Indian Ocean. Pakistan has also served as China's main link with the Muslim world.

The period between 1980 and 1990 witnessed an improvement in relations between India and China. Pakistan viewed the Sino-India reconciliation as a potential impediment to its relations with China. But, despite a thaw in India-China relations, the fundamentals of China-Pakistan relationship remained strong. Chinese neutrality on anti-India issues like the case of Kashmir was visible. During the rapprochement phase, Beijing directed its efforts to disentangle itself from the India-Pakistan conflict which was regarded important in order to ensure better Sino-Indian relations. The change was visible post-1990 when China adopted a neutral position on Kashmir as opposed to its stand which advocated support for Pakistan from 1964 to 1990. However, there was no difference in their relations. During this period China assisted Pakistan in the construction of the heavy water Khushab reactor, which till date remains critical for the production of plutonium and tritium for advanced compact warheads in Pakistan. Other forms of assistance comprised projects like reprocessing, conversion, production reactors, etc. The Chinese practice of supplying Pakistan with conventional and critical technologies like missile remained unchanged throughout the reconciliation phase with India and as always, Pakistan endorsed

China's stand on sensitive issues like Tibet, Taiwan, Hong Kong and human rights. After the withdrawal of Soviet Union from Afghanistan, Pakistan lost its relevance to the USA. Following the withdrawal, Pakistan became a victim of US sanctions for covertly undertaking development of nuclear weapons. From there on China replaced US as Pakistan's strategic ally and Sino-Pakistan defence oriented cooperation got further entrenched. Throughout 1990s, China was responsible for filling up Pakistan's military requirements through conventional, nuclear and missile technologies.

After the disintegration of USSR, China turned its attention towards India which now became vulnerable due to the disintegration of its ally. Meanwhile, Pakistan started looking for newer avenues for the supply of military hardware after being slapped by the Pressler Amendment in October 1990. The most tempting offer was to look to China for assistance. The momentum of nuclear supplies and arms transfers gained strength in the 1990s. The construction of Chashma nuclear plant in Pakistan commenced in 1992 by the Chinese aid. Other proliferation issues included the supply of missiles and support for Pakistan's nuclear weapons programme. Two momentous events at the end of the 1990s further strengthened China's resolve to strengthen Pakistan against India. India surprised the world after it conducted a series of nuclear tests on May 11 and 13, 1998. China's nuclear assistance to Pakistan was evident as Pakistan followed India by carrying out five nuclear tests.

During the Kargil War, China remained neutral and it was seen as a shift from its previous position. Pakistan's misadventure was drawing international condemnation and it hoped that China would be more sympathetic overtly. However, the Chinese actions on the world stage did not meet Pakistani expectations. China expressed hopes that India and Pakistan would find a solution through negotiations. China also advised Pakistan to exercise restraint. However, China made a demonstrative support for Pakistan by heightening its activities along the Sino-India border in Arunachal Pradesh. Chinese activities were also evident in Ladakh area along the LAC which coincided with the beginning of the Kargil War. The

Kargil War showed that the Chinese practice of pressurizing India by its actions on the second front was still prevalent. It is believed by the analysts that Chinese involvement restricted India from going into a full blown conflict with Pakistan. China did not get directly engaged in the conflict and earned a positive global reputation for not taking sides. As compared to the earlier Indo-Pak wars, China's diplomatic support and statements containing warnings for India were missing during the Kargil conflict, thereby indicating a change in China's position on Pakistan-related issues. Suffering from the threat of fundamentalism in its own restive Xinjiang province, China's overt support to Pakistan could have increased problems at home. However, this gave an opportunity to India to improve its relations with the US.

During Operation Parakram, Pakistan urged China to ease tensions with India by influencing Russia. As always, during Operation Parakram, Chinese maintained pressure in the eastern sector which prevented any possibility of diversion of Indian troops towards Pakistan. China was also involved in adding Pakistan's military assets. It is reported that in early December 2001, China discreetly sent ships to Pakistan carrying unassembled combat aircrafts and other air force-related weapons and equipment. Chinese assistance resulted in adding several squadrons of brand new Super-7 and F-7 fighter aircraft narrowing the ratio of air forces between India and Pakistan. Also, spares and other equipment for strategic assets were delivered through the Karakoram Highway. Even though China urged Pakistan not get involved in a war and divert its attention to economic development, it affirmed that once Pakistan was invaded, China would firmly stand on its side.

World order witnessed a change after the 9/11 attacks on America. Pakistan came under immense pressure from the US to become a frontline state in the Global War on Terrorism and was compelled to delink itself from the terrorist groups. With no space to manoeuvre, Pakistan was forced to comply with the wishes of USA. USA rewarded Pakistan for its cooperation by lifting economic and military sanctions and offering it aid, which greatly benefitted Pakistan's sinking economy. Entry of US in Afghanistan was not viewed positively by the Chinese who feared that increasing American presence would loosen China's hold on the Central Asian Republics. Despite the fears, China could understand Pakistan's limitations in dealing with the US pressure. China expressed its support for Pakistan. China mediated between Washington and Islamabad asking the US to help Pakistan economically at the crucial time. In order to assure Pakistan, China moved its troops towards the Pakistan-Afghanistan border, a move which was designed to reassure Pakistan of the proximity of Chinese forces.

2002 saw a change in China's internal politics. Arrival of new leadership, growing influence in international, economic and security affairs gave confidence to China. China now started speaking more of its increased assertiveness and sensitivities with regard to its core interests.Resultant was further growing of ties with Pakistan. The period witnessed strong defence cooperation. In 2004, both agreed to build a 300MW nuclear power plant at Chashma in Pakistan. The deal was signed despite international pressure and scrutiny. A motivating factor for enhanced Sino-Pakistan partnership was India's growing closeness to the US. China's rise and its potential to challenge the superpower prompted USA to strengthen its strategic ties with India as a counter balance to China in South Asia. Perceiving US friendship with India as a part of the strategy of encirclement, China revived its partnership with Pakistan. This was personified in the Sino-Pak Treaty of Friendship, Cooperation and Good-neighbourly Relations, which was signed and ratified by both sides on April 5, 2005 and January 4, 2006 respectively. Both countries vowed against joining any alliance or bloc which infringed upon the sovereignty, security and territorial integrity of the other side. Pakistan reiterated its one-China stance and both agreed to cooperate on terrorism. This treaty illustrates the closest China and Pakistan have come to an official alliance. However, there was a difference in perception by both the countries as Pakistan was looking towards China to defend its sovereignty, independence and territorial integrity. The difference of emphasis on both sides demonstrated Pakistan's eagerness to openly ally with China against its enemy and Chinese reluctance to portray the understanding of an alliance. China's hesitation in forming a formal alliance with Pakistan was conspicuous. China meanwhile had started encountering Muslim fundamentalism in its Xinjiang province. Reports indicated that these secessionists used assistance provided by hard core fundamentalist groups present in North West Pakistan. This imposed a caution in China's approach towards Pakistan. Also, China felt that a formal alliance with Pakistan would undo the flexibility PRC has always enjoyed. The disinclination towards openly acknowledging its understanding with Pakistan shows how China wants to grow with increased assertiveness yet not irk other powers to a level that can be considered dangerous for its rise. In spite of these reservations the period saw the fruition of the first phase of the strategic Gwadar Port, which can be seen as an important achievement of Sino-Pakistan relations and can also be regarded as China's door way to the Middle East. The US–India Civil Nuclear Agreement which was inked in 2008 created ripples in South Asia and called for stronger Sino-Pak ties to challenge India's power backed by the US. This development was viewed very seriously by the Chinese government. China proposed a similar deal to Pakistan, which was initially refused by the US.With the announcement of the Indo-US nuclear deal, there was a growing sense of assertiveness by China. Chinese assertive attitude manifested itself in numerous issues ranging from its take on Arunachal Pradesh to its policies in Kashmir.

26/11 attack in Mumbai witnessed a condemnation by the world. China's duality was once again displayed in 26/11. China's instant reaction to the attack was strong condemnation and condolences for the bereaved families and dead. With ensuing investigations tracing the attackers' link to Pakistan, the strains between India and Pakistan were conspicuous. China was quick to help Pakistan by attempting to diffuse the situation by appealing both countries to strengthen dialogue and bilateral cooperation. Analysts feel that China's non-admission of the angle of elements within Pakistan ascertained its pro-Pakistan bias which was contrary to its stand on terrorist attacks by Pakistan-trained Uighur militants in Xinjiang.

As India and the US come closer, the consequences can be traced in China and Pakistan's strategic posture and diplomatic attitude towards India and US. This resulted in a shift in China's strategy towards India. Its approach towards the Indo – Pak Kashmir problem underwent a strategic shift and the dispute which was seen as a bilateral one was now being perceived as a trilateral dispute. Since 2008, China has been refusing to paste regular visas to residents of Jammu and Kashmir and instead staple loose sheets, which are not recognised by the Indian government. The practice has continued despite repeated opposition from India. A similar move by China compelled India to cancel its defence exchanges in 2010, after it refused visa to India's Northern Army Commander. It stated reason was that the officer controlled Jammu and Kashmir, a state that China considers disputed.

Sino- Pak relations were strengthened due to the US involvement in South Asia. This was most advertised after the killing of Osama bin Laden in May 2011. China was the first country that expressed its support for the Pakistan. Fifteen days after the event, Pakistan PM made a four-day long official visit to China. At that time, China decided to expedite the delivery of 50 JF-17 fighter aircrafts, fully funded by China to boost Pakistan's defence capability. Since the 2011 raid, Pakistan's ties with USA are on a brink and will naturally die down following the proposed US withdrawal from Afghanistan. Pakistan has since publicised the Sino-Pakistan ties to show that it is not without trusted friends.

Despite China's support for Pakistan in the political, economic and strategic domains, there has been reluctance to offer Pakistan more than what China thinks it deserves. The most important and undeniable reality of Sino-Pakistan relations is that China's assistance to Pakistan is dependent on strategic designs and not emotions. China being the bigger player in the equation calls the shots and employs Pakistan as a military deterrent against India.

It is undeniable that the US aid to Pakistan in terms of economy and military aid is unparalleled. While China may have crossed the US supplies mark during the years of sanctions, this does not hold true when analysing the complete range of assistance bestowed by the Americans on Pakistan. It is also doubtful that China would abandon Pakistan like the USA. A likely prediction of Sino-Pak strategic collaboration is that China would continue to support Pakistan's military which would always remain at the core of their ties. The importance of Pakistan's military and geography for China surpasses all other areas of convergences with its South Asian friend, which will be greatly utilised to further China's ambitions. China's bond with Pakistan has allowed the former a greater sphere of influence in to South Asia, as well provided a bridge between the Muslim world and China. Though, traditionally, the driving factor for China was a hedge against India and getting strategic leverage against India, relations with China gave Pakistan access to civilian and military resources also. To this day, the collaboration between the two countries is of high strategic importance, the military relationship with China being the corner stone of Pakistan's foreign policy. And in return, Pakistan is helpful in realising China's dream of establishing her influence over the globe.

2 | MILITARY COLLABORATION

Genesis

Sino-Pak relationship is primarily military-driven with sprinkling of economic aspect. Armed forces of both countries have developed an enduring but unequal partnership in which China is the larger beneficiary. Pakistan's strategic conduct is heavily shaped by presumptions of unconditional Chinese support. Although contradicted in reality, such presumptions have led Pakistan to pursue adventurous policies against India. The armed forces of both countries have striking similarities and are infused with a strong sense of historical grievances against the West and India. Both suffer from a phobia of perceived harm by foreign powers due to their economic and nuclear capabilities. Both believe in authoritarian regimes and are against the institution of democracy.

Beginning of the military collaboration dates back to the 1950s when the Pakistan Army undertook several studies of People's Warfare, at the advice of USA. What began as an effort to understand the dangers of communist subversion, made Pakistani military policy makers appreciate the positive contribution that such subversion could make in degrading an enemy's war-fighting potential. This resulted in fostering a long lasting admiration for communist China. In the latter half of the decade, Pakistan clandestinely opened an air corridor for China thereby allowing it to bypass international trade embargo. Therefore, Sino-Pak military collaboration pre-dated the 1962 Sino-Indian War. Probably China and Pakistan realized that peaceful coexistence amidst conflicting territorial claims was impossible. 1960's saw a change in Pakistan's attitude towards China. The earlier aristocracy and landlord class of army officers were now replaced by officers from middle and poor background having strong Islamist views. This brought a change in their attitude towards West. The second development was Bhutto, a populist politician with strong leftist sympathies. Bhutto reportedly urged Pakistan's military dictator, Ayub Khan, to attack India in 1962, when the Indian Army was preoccupied with responding to a PLA attack from Tibet. Under pressure from the United States, Ayub Khan resisted this advice. He did however, open talks with Beijing over the status of Pakistan's own disputed Kashmir frontier with China. A settlement was quickly reached; resulting in the removal of what was then the only major irritant in the Sino-Pak relationship. In reaching this settlement, Pakistan back tracked on its own stand that the status of Kashmir should be decided between India and Pakistan, before any consideration was given to Chinese territorial claims. Bhutto was the leading advocate of closer Sino-Pak cooperation. He was already inclined to be cynical of the alliance with the United States and projected its decision to supply military aid to India in 1962 as a betrayal to Pakistan. Encouraged by the Indian's poor performance against China, he strongly supported Pakistan's 1965 military offensive into Indian Kashmir.

The failure of Pakistan's 1965 offensive brought home the harsh reality that outside help would be needed to fight India. With the West having imposed an arms embargo on both countries and Pakistan having already aligned against the Soviet Union, the only plausible candidate was China. For its part, owing to the Sino-Soviet split, Beijing too was in need of allies. During the active phase of Indo-Pak hostilities, it had provided rhetorical support to the Pakistani attack and made signs of opening a second front along the Indo-Tibet border. Although Chinese assistance never went beyond words, Pakistan's security establishment became permanently obliged for it. Helping Pakistan to confront India seemed to be a logical option for the Chinese leadership. It also ensured security along China's Tibetan frontier at little direct cost.

The 1971 Indo - Pak war was another occasion for China to offer support to Islamabad. It's assistance to Pakistan was kept up by a constant supply of material, verbal and moral support throughout the crisis. Some movement of Chinese troops was also reported during the time; however it did not restrict Indian military actions in East Pakistan. The moves were as in 1965 designed to pressurize India psychologically and earn goodwill of Pakistan. Pakistan's expectations of a direct Chinese involvement in East Pakistan did not materialize. Post-1971, China made all attempts to replenish Pakistan's defence power and helped improve its economic situation in addition to offering immense moral and symbolic support. A highpoint came in 1972, when China used its veto power to block the admission of Bangladesh as a new UN member. China facilitated the release of Pakistani POWs and got troops reverted to pre-war positions. The period stretching from 1971 to 1978 saw exceptional Chinese assistance in defence-infrastructure projects and a variety of military equipment without attaching any strings. From 1971 to 1978, China assisted Pakistan in building two defence-related mega projects, first was the Heavy Industries Taxila and its part Heavy Rebuild Factory for T-59 tanks and second was the F-6 Aircraft Rebuild Factory.

In 1974 India conducted its first nuclear test. This development was a major turning point in China-Pak relations which accelerated China's military assistance to Pakistan. As the end of 1970s neared, global events re-shaped the landscape of South Asia. The region witnessed greater instability with the commencement of the Iranian revolution in early 1979 and the invasion of Afghanistan by the erstwhile Soviet Union. Pakistan and China felt uncomfortable with Soviet aggression close to their border. The development particularly affected Pakistan as for the first time it brought an extra regional threat at its doorstep. With strategic priorities converging yet again, China supported Pakistan's move to ally with the US and wage a covert war against USSR in Afghanistan. China employed Pakistan as a proxy and granted covert military supplies worth US $ 200 million to the Afghan resistance movement. This also witnessed an increased cooperation in defence and nuclear fields. American engagement and its need for Pakistan's geographical positioning posed a perfect opportunity for it to embark on its nuclear programme with Chinese assistance. This decade saw a high frequency of exchanges in the top civil and military level for consultations to gain an understanding of each other's stance on bilateral relations and global affairs.

The period between 1980 and 1990 witnessed an improvement in relations between India and China. Pakistan viewed the Sino-India reconciliation as a potential impediment to its relations with China. But, despite a thaw in India-China relations, the fundamentals of China-Pakistan relationship remained strong. During this period China assisted Pakistan in the construction of the heavy water Khushab reactor, which till date remains critical for the production of plutonium and tritium for advanced compact warheads in Pakistan. Other forms of assistance comprised projects like reprocessing, conversion, production reactors, etc. The Chinese practice of supplying Pakistan with conventional and critical technologies like missiles remained unchanged throughout their conciliation phase with India. After the withdrawal of Soviet Union from Afghanistan, Pakistan lost its relevance to the USA. From there on China replaced US as Pakistan's strategic ally and Sino-Pakistan defence oriented cooperation got further entrenched. Throughout 1990s, China was responsible for filling up Pakistan's military requirements through conventional, nuclear and missile technologies.

The most important link between the militaries of China and Pakistan is also economic; the 1300 km long Karakoram Highway. Construction of this highway began in 1966, one year after Pakistan's abortive military offensive against India and it was opened in 1982. Less than a year later, Pakistan cold-tested a nuclear device and subsequently acquired blueprints for a nuclear bomb from China. Beijing supplied nuclear-capable missiles to Islamabad via the Karakoram Highway, besides outfitting the Pakistani Army with conventional weaponry. The Karakoram Highway is currently being maintained in part by Chinese engineering troops based in Pakistani territory. At least 16 tactical airstrips have been constructed along the highway, which is being expanded from its current width of 10 meters to 30 meters. In the event of a war with India, Pakistan's strategic airlift capabilities would be enhanced by these upgrades. It is interesting to note that this period (the early and mid-1980s) coincided with the beginning of massive and systemic Pak support to insurgent groups in India's Punjab province. The Karakoram Highway was crucial in augmenting the Pakistani military's strength and enabling Islamabad to pursue a covert war against India. Beginning in Punjab, this war expanded to Jammu and Kashmir in 1989 and to rest of India in 1993, when multiple bomb blasts took place across Mumbai. Indian analysts suggest that, once it had acquired a nuclear umbrella and substantial quantities of Chinese weapons, Pakistan lost all inhibitions about escalating hostilities through proxy warfare. Despite its military character, in recent years the Karakoram Highway has adopted the additional role of being an economic connector. The presence of Chinese troops in POK indicates its de facto acceptance of Pakistan's claim over the area.

The momentum of nuclear supplies and arms transfers gained strength in the 1990s. Construction of Chashma nuclear plant in Pakistan was commenced in 1992 by the Chinese. Other proliferation issues included the supply of M-11 missiles and support for Pakistan's nuclear weapons programme. It was also during this stage that the China-Pakistan-North Korea axis developed, which added to the levels of illicit proliferation of arms and defence related technologies. India conducted a series of nuclear tests on May 11 and 13, 1998 at Pokhran which further strengthened China's resolve to strengthen Pakistan against India.

1999 saw the Kargil War between India and Pakistan. In spite of neutral statements on Kargil, China made a demonstration of support for Pakistan by heightening its activities on the Sino-India border in Arunachal Pradesh and Ladakh. The Kargil War indicated that the Chinese practice of pressurizing India by its actions on the second front was still prevalent. Chinese involvement is always believed to have made the stakes for India higher. Going by a probable Chinese calculation, its involvement in the Kargil crisis could have averted a full-blown war, thereby helping Pakistan. As always, China did not get directly engaged in an Indo-Pak conflict and also earned a positive reputation for not taking sides.

During the Operation Parakram, Pakistan urged China to ease tensions with India by influencing Russia. As always, during Operation Parakram, Chinese maintained pressure in the eastern sector which prevented any possibility of diversion of Indian troops towards Pakistan. China was also involved in adding Pakistan's military assets. Chinese assistance resulted in adding several squadrons of brand new Super-7 and F-7 fighter aircraft narrowing the ratio of air forces between India and Pakistan. Also, spares and other equipment for strategic assets were delivered through the Karakoram Highway.

2002 saw a change in leadership in China which can be termed as the fourth generation leadership led by Hu Jintao. The arrival of new generation leadership became visible in China's foreign and security policies. There was a new sense of confidence in the Chinese leadership which can be attributed to its growing economic and military clout. There was a drastic change in its actions which showed increased assertiveness and sensitivities with regard to China's core interests. The period also saw a growing closeness between USA and India which was a motivating factor for enhanced Sino-Pak partnership. The US–India Civil Nuclear Agreement which was inked in 2008 called for a stronger Sino-Pak collaboration to challenge India's power backed by the US. This development was viewed very seriously by the Chinese government. They also went ahead to propose a similar deal with Pakistan. China started showing its assertiveness towards India on issues related to Arunachal Pradesh and Kashmir.

After the US raid that killed Osama bin Laden, Pakistan faced criticism from the international community. China was the first country that expressed its support for its ally praising its important contributions in international counter-terrorism cooperation. China decided to expedite the delivery of 50 JF-17 fighter aircrafts, fully funded by China to boost Pakistan's defence capability. Since the 2011 raid, Islamabad's ties with Washington are on a decline. Pakistan has since then publicized its ties with China to show that it is not without trusted friends. China being the bigger player in the equation calls the shots and employs Pakistan as a military deterrent against India doing what the PLA should have done. Pakistan cannot ever consider China subservient to its needs.

Manifestation of Military Collaboration

Pakistan Army

Heavy Rebuild Factory, Taxila. Heavy Rebuild Factory was constructed in 1980 at Taxila in collaboration with China. This factory overhauls Chinese built T-59 tanks and also carries out licensed production of Chinese Type-60 II BMPs.Once Pakistan had gained expertise in rebuilding Chinese tanks, the complex was transformed into a massive defence complex and was renamed as Heavy Industries Taxila (HIT). HIT has produced Al- Zarrar (upgraded variant of the Chinese Type 59 tank, Tank T-59MII, Tank T-69IIMP, Tank T-85IIAP, ARV W-563, SP Gun M109A2/ M110A2, Al-Khalid/MBT-2000/Type 90-IIM, APC M113 A1/A2, 125 mm Tank Gun Barrel, APC M113 A2 MK– 1.HIT comprises of various defence factories specialize in refurbishing, rebuilding and development of MBT, ARV, APCs and other A Vehicles of eastern and western origin. A gun factory has also been established in collaboration with the Chinese in1994 and has been producing gun barrels for the upgraded T-59 & T-69 tanks.

Arms Transfer. After the US sanctions in1990s, China has become the major arms provider for Pakistan. As per the Stockholm International Peace Research Institute (SIPRI), Pakistan has purchased 55 percent of China's weapons exports in the years 2008 to 2012. A variety of military equipment to include tanks, anti-tank missiles, air defence guns and radars, MRLs, artillery weapon systems (122 mm How Type 59, 122mm How D30,122mm MBRL etc) and bridging equipment have been purchased. China has been providing interest free credit facility to Pakistan since 1981 where in the repayment is made in 10 instalments. In view of Pakistan's poor economy, this has provided an impetus to procurement of Chinese origin arms and equipment.

Joint Training. Since 2003, China and Pakistan have held numerous joint and multilateral exercises. These joint exercises have resulted in a high degree of inter-operability among the armed forces. Interestingly, some of these exercises have been conducted close to the border with India i.e in Suryaan and Chor, near Sem Nala in Rahim Yaar Khan in Pakistan, adjoining Tanot-Kishangarh in Jaisalmer. As per analysts, it appears that China was assisting Pakistan in India's western sector and the game may be a way to put pressure on India through the Pakistan border. In addition to joint conventional training, emphasis has given to counter terrorist operations thereby indicating China's sensitivity to its Muslim dominated areas in Xinjiang Uygur Autonomous Region. These training events have been participated by company, battalion and brigade level troops from both sides.

Pakistan Air Force

China – Pakistan collaborations in supply of aircrafts and technology commenced after the 1965 Indo – Pak war. China has been seen as a reliable partner, willing to supply defence items at cheap rates with easy payment options. The first supply included 73 F-6 fighter aircrafts which were inducted in December 1965. The supply of aircrafts include F-7M Airguard fighter aircraft, Y-12 transport aircrafts, F-7MG fighters, A-5C Fantan FGA aircraft, AS-565SA Panther AWS helicopters KJ-200 AEW & C aircrafts, J-10/FC-20 FGA aircrafts, k-8 trainer/combat aircrafts, Z9EC helicopters and JF-17 Thunder FGA aircrafts. PAF had been keeping a track of India's intentions of acquiring a fleet of Multi-Role Combat Aircraft (MRCA). As a result of this PAF was eyeing early induction of JF-17, AEW&C capabilities and acquisition of Chinese-built FC-20/J-10B Multirole combat aircraft. PAF finally received the JF-17 Thunder series in 2009 and 2011. The JF-17 aircraft is a prized possession for the air force for it provides the much desired air-to-air and air-to-ground weapon carrying capability at an affordable cost. Interestingly, the 2011 batch of JF-17 was a result of China expediting the delivery of 50 aircraft (given free of cost) in the wake of the killing of Osama bin Laden, following which Pakistan was under immense criticism from the international community. The delivery of these aircrafts has strengthened PAF's air defence capabilities and has shown the Chinese support to Pakistan in times of crisis. PAF plans to induct almost 150 JF-17 aircrafts till 2020.

Another area of interest for Pakistan has been to possess AEW&C, for which China has always been a readily available supplier. The PAF felt the need to acquire AEW&C aircraft after the Kargil war. In 2008, China and Pakistan entered into negotiations to procure four ZDK-03 'Karakoram Eagle' (AEW&C) aircraft. The aircraft is equipped with advanced integrated sensors and communications suite which would enhance PAF's detection and interception capabilities.The first aircraft was received by the PAF in November 2010, which made Pakistan the first nation to buy Chinese AEW&C aircraft.

Pakistan Aeronautical Complex, Kamra. Chinese F-6 fighters were inducted in the Pakistani Air Force in 1966. Over the time it was realized that no overhauling could not be undertaken due to non-existence of a facility in Pakistan. Under the supervision of the Chinese specialists, the foundation of a facility was laid at Kamra and the first aircraft was built in 1974. The factory was named as Aircraft Rebuild Factory (ARF) or as formerly referred as F-6 Rebuild Factory (F-6RF). China provided the establishment with latest technical facilities and machines for numerous engineering processes. ARF has handled the overhauling and manufacturing of parts for Shenyang F-6, FT-5, FT-6 jet trainer aircraft, Nanchang A-5 and F-7 combat aircraft. The complex is dedicated to servicing, assembly and production of aircrafts, space systems and UAVs. The complex consists of factories such as Aircraft Rebuild Factory, Mirage Rebuild Factory, Aircraft Manufacturing Factory and Kamra Avionics and Radar Factory (KARF).

Aircraft Manufacturing Factory (AMF). The Aircraft Manufacturing Factory (AMF) is the pivotal arm of PAC as it embarks on the manufacturing of heavy defence aircrafts. Its first venture was the production of MFI-17 Mushshak, which were used PAF and Pakistan Army Aviation. AMF has provided a platform to Pakistan and China to pursue joint production ventures such as K-8 Karakorum/Hongdu JL-8 intermediate/advanced jet trainer and Joint Fighter JF-17/Chengdu FC-1/Super-7. In addition to the factories mentioned earlier, Kamra Avionics and Radar Factory (KARF) is another facility that is responsible for manufacture of Pakistan's radar systems. In 1983, the Radar Maintenance Centre (RMC) was set up in partnership with the Chinese, to assemble service and rebuild ground-based radar systems, electronics and avionics. Expanding it role and responsibilities, RMC was renamed as Kamra Radar & Avionics Factory (KARF). A comprehensive unit for avionics maintenance was integrated into KARF. KARF in the present times is capable of testing, inspecting and repairing all types of data, power and Radio Frequency (RF) cables.

Joint Training. PAF and PLA Air Force (PLAAF) have participated in joint exercises- Shaheen-1(2011) and Shaheen- 2(Sep 2013). These exercises between the two air forces have resulted in greater understanding of each other to enable interoperability and jointness.

Pakistan Navy

Sino-Pak naval cooperation grew after the 1971 Indo-Pak war due to Western sanctions on Pakistan. The Pakistani Navy comprised of vintage warships and lacked effective and agile naval platforms. To plug this capability gap, China proceeded to supply naval craft of various types to Pakistan, which joined its Navy in batches throughout the 70s and early 80s. These included Huchuan class fast attack hydrofoil craft, Hainan class submarine chasers, Shanghai-II class fast patrol/gun boats, Huang Fen class fast attack missile craft and Hegn class fast attack missile craft. They added a new dimension to the Pakistan Navy (PN) fleet and enabled it to effectively carry out surveillance of its southeast sector along the Pakistani coast whose vulnerability was exposed during the 1971 war. By 1984, the entire flotilla of promised Chinese ships had been integrated into the PN. The successful experience of Chinese naval platforms reiterated the PN's confidence in China's naval hardware, prompting Pakistan to venture into acquisition of larger naval vessels. A bilateral agreement was signed for the construction of 20,000 tons fleet replenishment tanker in early 1986. The ship was constructed according to the navy's requirements and commissioned as PNS NASR in August 1987.

In the 1990s, the slapping of Pressler Amendment on Pakistan by the US impelled its defence planners to seek further Beijing's assistance and cooperation in the field of naval construction and aim for indigenization. This led to construction and induction of missile craft. Besides undertaking bilateral naval visits, the relationship blossomed in 2005 when the deal to acquire four F-22P frigates under Transfer of Technology (ToT) package was signed with China. Under this agreement, three ships were to be constructed in China, while the fourth one in Pakistan with Chinese assistance. These ships are designed to operate in multi-threat environment and are fitted with sophisticated sensors suite and weapons. They also carry Z-9EC helicopters that have been delivered to the PN, enhancing its anti-submarine warfare capabilities. PN also signed a deal under ToT with China in 2011 for the construction of two fast missile crafts. They were to be constructed one each at China and Pakistan and would also carry advanced missiles capable of hitting targets at extended ranges. In addition, Pakistan Navy has signed a deal with China for the induction of radar controlled guns and low level air defence radars for the terminal air defence of its vital installations. To replace its ageing submarine fleet ones, Pakistan is actively involved with China in acquisition discussions. In 2011, reports emerged confirming Pakistan's order of six Qing class submarines from China. These submarines are equipped with air independent propulsion (AIP) system, which would give them capability to stay submerged longer and operate noiselessly. The agreement includes co-production and development in which four submarines will be built in China and two in Pakistan. The agreement also caters for training of Pak Navy personnel and upgradation of Pakistan Navy shipyard. As per the reports there is a possibility of these submarines capable of carrying nuclear warheads, which is fulfills Pakistan's dream of owning a nuclear submarine. More importantly, Qing is likely to carry almost three nuclear capable CJ-10K surface to surface missiles, with a range of 1500 kms. This procurement clearly reflects Pakistan's attempt to establish a sea-based minimum credible nuclear deterrent against India. The deal is being accorded priority by Pakistan due to induction of nuclear-powered ballistic missile submarine (SSBN) INS Arihant by India. Another high point of Sino-Pak naval collaboration has been China's assistance in the construction of Gwadar Port which provides an opportunity to China in maintaining a strong regional influence in the Arabian Sea and ensuring the security of its SLOCs.

Joint Training. Both the countries have carried out joint training since 2003. The first exercise was the Dolphin 0310 which was conducted in China. In November 2005, Pakistan and China conducted second joint naval exercise, China-Pakistan Friendship 2005, in the Arabian Sea off the Karachi coast. This was China's first military drill in alien sea waters. The third exercise was the AMAN 2007 which was a multinational exercise conducted by Pakistan Navy and attended by the PLAN. This was followed by AMAN 2009 and AMAN 2011. In March 2013, Pakistan has conducted another multinational maritime joint exercise Peace–1 which has been participated by PLAN's 14th Escort Taskforce. The exercise consisted two parts: the coast and port special operation forces' drills and the ship-aircraft joint maritime drills.

Over the years, defence forces of both the countries have been involved in various facets of joint training which has added a new dimension to their military collaboration. It has resulted in understanding each other's war-fighting methods and interoperability issues. The implications of Sino – Pak military collaboration for India and the region are as follows:-

- Cooperation between the two countries is likely to intensify after thinning of US presence in the Af-Pak region.

- China and Pakistan will want to play a dominant role in South Asia.

- Due to the deepening bonds between China and Pakistan and increased presence of Chinese troops in Pakistan, it will force China to bail out Pakistan in case of emergencies.

- Pakistan will continue to see China as a reliable and dependent partner in terms of arms supplies, especially during contingencies.

- Beijing and Islamabad will continue to undertake collaborative efforts in R&D and manufacturing of weapon systems which will lead to further arms race in the region.

MISSILE COLLABORATION

Pakistan's efforts towards missile development became prominent in early 1960s when it began working on nurturing its rocketry expertise, which paved way for its missile programme. The missile programme was officially embarked upon after the establishment of Space and Upper Atmosphere Research Commission (SUPARCO) in 1981. China began discussing possible sales of M-11 missiles and related technology to Pakistan in the late 1980s. The contract for M-11 sale was reportedly signed in 1988. In April 1991, United States announced that it had discovered the transfer of an M-11 missile even though China insisted it had never shipped the system to Pakistan. In May 1991, US imposed sanctions against China. In September 1992 US decision to sell 150 F-16 fighters to Taiwan led China to withdraw from P-5 talks on conventional arms transfers. In December 1992 reports surfaced that China had transferred 34 complete M-11 systems to Pakistan. China and Pakistan both denied that the transfer had taken place.

In August 1993, the Clinton Administration imposed MTCR related sanctions on China after determining that China had again engaged in missile trade with Pakistan. China denounced the sanctions, calling the US decision "a wrong judgment based on inaccurate intelligence" and threatened to scrap its promise to abide by the MTCR. The impasse was finally over in October 1994 when the two countries issued a joint statement on missile proliferation. In the joint statement, the United States agreed to lift sanctions and in return China promised to ban all exports of ground-to-ground missiles exceeding the primary parameters of the MTCR. China also agreed to accept the concept of "inherent capability" which binds China from exporting any missile that is inherently capable of delivering a 500 kg payload over 300 km. This standard would prohibit future exports of the M-11 missile. The US waived the sanctions in November 1994.

China has also assisted Pakistan by including North Korea, which bartered its missiles for nuclear material and designs from Pakistan. In 1996, Taiwan and Hong Kong confiscated shipments containing Ammonium Perchlorate (AP), a solid-propellant component that was sent from North Korea via China to Pakistan. Pakistan's medium range ballistic missile (MRBM) Hatf- 5 or Ghauri which was first tested in 1998 is based on the technology of North Korea's No-Dong 1 and 2 missiles. The missile's guidance system was reportedly developed and provided by China through North Korea. Apart from this, Pakistan's Hatf-3 or Ghaznavi is nothing more than Chinese M-11 missiles. Pakistan's original plan to develop this missile got terminated in 1994 after China supplied numerous M-11 missiles to it. US intelligence reports suggest that the Shaheen-1 IRBM, which Pakistan tested in April 1999, is actually modelled on Chinese M-9 missiles. As per the inputs available with CIA and open sources, the scope of Sino – Pak missile collaboration is as given below:-

Missile System	Characteristics	Areas of Reported Chinese Assistance to Pakistan
M-11/DF-11/CSS-7 (reason for US sanctions against China in 1991 and 1993)	• Range: 300 km • Payload: 800 kg • Solid propellant • A few may be armed with nuclear warheads	• Chinese transfer of M-11 test missile and launcher (1991) • Direct transfers of 34 complete M-11s (1992) • Chinese provision of M-11 components and technology (1992, 1995) • Chinese missile technicians visited Pakistan M-11 sites (1994) • Chinese training of Pakistani M-11 army units (1995) • Reports of Chinese assistance with indigenous Pakistani M-11 production (1996-1997)
Establishment of missile factory for manufacture of medium-range ballistic missiles, likely the M-11 or a similar missile	• Located in Rawalpindi • Unclear whether this facility will be able to manufacture complete missiles or only some major components	Continuing Chinese assistance, including blueprints and construction equipment (1996-1997)

Missile System	Characteristics	Areas of Reported Chinese Assistance to Pakistan
Hatf-1/1A	• Range: 80 km (Haft-1A: 100 km) • Payload: 500 kg • Single stage; solid propellant	Possibly developed with some Chinese assistance
Hatf-2 (Abdali)	• Range: 300 km • Payload: 500 kg • Two stage; solid propellant	Possibly developed with some Chinese assistance
Hatf-VII(Babur) Cruise Missile	• Range : 700 km • Nuclear capable	Chinese assistance
Shaheen I &II	• Range: 750-2000KM • Payload: 850kg	• Possibly similar to China's M-9 • Nuclear and HE
Ammonium Perchlorate(AP)	Chemical used in rocket fuel	Alleged illegal Chinese shipment of 10 tons to Pakistan (1996)
Anza	Surface-to-air missile (SAM)	Pakistani version of PRC-supplied SAM

Missile System	Characteristics	Areas of Reported Chinese Assistance to Pakistan
Arms Materials	Special metals and electronics used in the production of Chinese-design anti-tank missiles (Pakistan's Baktar Shikhan is virtually identical to China's Red Arrow 8 guided missile)	Alleged Chinese shipment to Pakistan (1998)
Ghauri I	• Range : 1500Km • Pay Load : 500-750 • Single Liquid	DPRK/PRC
Ghauri II	• Range :1500-2300 Km • Pay Load :700 • Two Liquid	• North Korea/China and also Saudi Arabia • Nuclear and HE
Ghauri III Ballistic Missile	• Range : 2,700-3,000 Km	Chinese assistance
Ghaznavi	• Range: 290 Km • Warhead : Nuclear, HE, Cluster, Thermobaric, Radio Frequency	Chinese assistance

In a report to the Congress in May 2004, the U.S. Department of Defence highlighted the major improvements that China has made to its air and missile defence systems over the past few years, including the development of an anti - radiation SAM [surface-to-air missile], most likely intended to target AWACS [Airborne Warning and Control System] aircraft and standoff jamming platforms. The report was referring specifically to the FT-2000, a Chinese anti-radiation surface-to-air missile system designed to counter electronic jamming aircraft, AWACS aircraft, and other air radiation wave targets. Developed and manufactured by the China National Precision Machinery Import and Export Corporation (CPMIEC) during the late 1990s, the FT-2000 is also believed to be capable of destroying tactical ballistic missiles, similar to the U.S. Patriot and the Russian S-300P systems on which it is based. At present, two versions exist, the mobile FT-2000 and the fixed-based FT-2000A. The FT-2000 is the direct result of a concerted effort by China to eliminate an inherent jamming vulnerability in medium and long-range surface-to-air missiles.

In addition to the mobile FT-2000, China has developed a fixed-based variant, the FT-2000A. According to a recent Chinese sales brochure, the FT-2000A has been equipped with passive radio frequency homing seekers. Each missile is armed with a 60 kg fragmentation warhead and has a range of 60 km and a maximum altitude of 18 km. Reports indicate that each FT-2000A battery consists of 12 missile launchers, each containing one missile, and a central control station. Since the FT-2000 is based on comprehensive systems such as the U.S. Patriot and the S-300P, it is no surprise that it too has anti-missile capabilities.

In October 2003, it was reported that China had closed a deal with Pakistan, to supply the latter with an unspecified number of FT-2000 missiles to counter India's early warning capabilities. The China-Pakistan deal followed India's own arrangement with Israel and Russia to install three Israeli Phalcon AWACS on Ilyushin Il-76 freighter aircraft, thus giving it an airborne early warning system. According to various news sources, shortly after India announced its acquisition of the Phalcon radars, Pakistan's air force Chief visited China and conveyed Pakistani President's wish to purchase an unspecified number of FT-2000s. The recent China-Pakistan arrangement may just be an attempt to maintain the delicate balance of power between India and Pakistan, both of which possess nuclear weapons.

In September 2013, Chandan Nandy in an article in The Times of India reported that China moved N-missiles and launchers via Karakoram highway to Pak in 2005. It was reported that a few days after China conducted atomic blasts in Tibet in March 2005 to divert the Yarlung Tsangpo or the Brahmaputra, Indian spy planes and satellites spotted the transport of nuclear missiles and suspected fissile material over the Karakoram highway connecting China with Pakistan. The *Times of India* had earlier reported China's ambitious plan to divert the course of the Brahmaputra from south to north in Tibet's Moutou and Great Bend regions in March 2005. But what made the transfer of nuclear missiles – possibly to locations within Pakistan – significant from the Indian perspective was the movement of road-mobile, short-range ballistic missiles, Dongfeng 11, also known as M-11 missiles via the Karakoram highway in 1995. As per the writer, highly classified Indian intelligence reports suggested that in March 2005, an important contingent of the People's Liberation Army, carrying 11 transporter erector launcher (TEL) laden with short-range nuclear missiles was photographed by spy planes of the National Technical Research Organization (NTRO) moving through the Karakoram Pass. The Indian security establishment estimated the PLA troops, led by a brigadier rank officer, numbering about 550. Typically, Chinese TELs are 16-wheeled that have integrated prime movers that can carry, elevate to firing position and launch or multiple missiles. These vehicles are employed to fire surface-to-air as well as surface-to-surface missiles. The Chinese TELs are compatible for firing the Dongfeng 11 and some of the missile's more improved and lethal versions that have been deployed in different parts of China and shared with Pakistan.

The movement of the TELs, believed to have been designed and built by the China Aerospace Science and Industry Corporation, which is the PLA's main mobile-missile producer, on the Karakoram highway took place just before the then Chinese premier Wen Jiabao's visit to Islamabad in April 2005 when the two countries signed the Treaty of Friendship and Cooperation. At that time, China had also agreed to establish a facility to produce land attack cruise missiles (LACMs) for the Pakistanis. Indian intelligence, according to National Security Council reports, also learnt that the LACMs were tested in September 2005 and were suspected to have been transported from China which helped the Pakistanis build a ballistic missile manufacturing facility near Rawalpindi for the Shaheen-1, a variant of the Dongfeng 9 Chinese missiles.

In 2005, India and Pakistan signed an agreement requiring both parties to provide advance notice of any ballistic missile tests. Since 2007, testing activity of the Ghauri and Shaheen missiles have slowed and the majority of new developments have appeared in cruise, rather than ballistic missile systems. Potential causes for this include India's investment in a ballistic missile defence system, the Ghauri and Shaheen missiles acquiring sufficient range and payload to target strategic locations in India, international pressure against intermediate- and long-range ballistic missile tests, and a shift in focus toward developing a tactical nuclear capability.

The 2005 inaugural test-flight of the Hatf-7/Babur cruise missile stunned many observers for its technological complexity and its undetected development. The extent of foreign assistance (Chinese) remains unclear — analysts identified design similarities with Chinese cruise missiles as well as American Tomahawk missiles, which previously crash-landed over Pakistan. In 2007, Pakistan test-fired the Hatf-8/Ra'ad cruise missile, adding air-launch missile capabilities to the Pakistan Air Force. While Pakistan officially claimed that NDC indigenously developed the Hatf-8, some believe that the modest range of the missile suggests foreign assistance by a country unwilling to contravene MTCR range and payload restrictions which implies that it could be assisted by China. Pakistan has test-fired the

Hatf-9/NASR, a short-range nuclear-capable ballistic missile in April 2011. Observers immediately speculated that the Hatf-9/NASR test indicated potential Pakistani intention to develop a tactical nuclear capability—an interest potentially motivated further by India's "Cold Start" doctrine.

Despite flight test successes, however, analysts remain skeptical about Pakistan's indigenous design and manufacturing capabilities. The lack of robust government-industry-university R&D linkages, a known dependence on foreign suppliers for key raw materials such as steel alloys, and the technological inexperience of private industry cast doubt upon Pakistan's missile design claims. While Pakistani scientists increasingly participate in basic science collaboration with foreign laboratories, such as the European Organization for Nuclear Research (CERN), the country's industrial base lacks a demonstrated history of producing quality high-tech products. A history of indigenous design claims refuted by intelligence sources further complicates assessments. Analysts estimate that even gaining liquid propulsion expertise will take considerable time. Thus, it is safe to assume that Pakistan's missile development is likely to be dependent on Chinese assistance for both materials and expertise in the near-term.

Sino – Pak Collusive Threat to India

Having analysed the military aspect of the strategic nexus between China and Pakistan, an attempt is now being made to examine the collusive threat these two nations pose to India.

Factors Leading to a Joint Threat to India

India has been the main factor that has influenced China's and Pakistan's policies towards each other. India faces a unique security scenario involving two nuclear-armed neighbours with whom it has not only been to war but who together also present a joint threat to its security. As mentioned earlier, other than posturing of troops and diplomatic noises, China has never participated actively in a conflict between India and Pakistan. Probably the reason could be that China did not have much to stake in terms of assets or interests in Pakistan. However, over the years its military footprints in the Northern areas of Pakistan and POK in disguise of construction activities have increased considerably. Millions of dollars are being used by China for the construction of the KKH which serves as an important road link that connects the Gwadar port to China's western border. POK also acts as a link for China's interests in Afghanistan. In Dec 2014, China stated that POK is a part of Pakistan.

The Chinese presence and interests in POK has added a new dimension to the long drawn Indo-Pak dispute over the state of Jammu and Kashmir. It has transformed the Kashmir dispute into a trilateral dispute with China being the third stake holder. It indicates that Pakistan is now a frontline state of China's grand strategy to strengthen its presence in South Asia. The Chinese involvement in POK can also be treated as a signal to India to abstain from interfering in matters related to Tibet. These developments now pose a Chinese threat to India not only along the LAC but also along the Line of Control. It will not be incorrect to state that China would be sensitive to any Indian threat to its interests in the area. Any Indian military action against Pakistan in areas having China's interests is likely to invite an active reaction from China which would manifest in a two front war for India. The Chinese development activities will facilitate speedy and enhanced deployment of Pakistan Army to complement China's military actions and thus be able to outflank India.

Ground Realities

Even though the combined Sino – Pak threat exists for India, however, at the diplomatic and economic front a different picture emerges. Historically China has never actively participated in an Indo – Pak conflict. It is visualized that in case of Indo – Pak conflict in future with focus on shallow gains by India not threatening China's interests in Pakistan, are not likely to invite a response by China.

The growing terrorism in China's Xinjiang province with credible proof of the militants being trained in Pakistan's Northern areas has made China cautious of its relationship with Pakistan. Its national security is more important than its all-weather friendship with Pakistan as the militancy in Xinjiang would have impact on Tibet also. Recent joint statement by China and Russia, to support India for moving a proposal at the UN to punish those who shelter and finance terrorism essentially goes against Pakistan. This is a rare occasion when China, a close ally of Pakistan, has taken a stand on an issue that is bound to rattle Islamabad. Beijing's move not only reflects the importance it accords to New Delhi, but is also an acknowledgment of its own problem of terrorism in Xinjiang province. Also, the growing diplomatic and economic engagements between China and India indicate a shift in China's policies towards India. Therefore, it can be assumed that China is not likely to present India with collusive threat with Pakistan. Notwithstanding the above, India should be prepared to meet such a threat in future.

3 | NUCLEAR COLLABORATION

Sino-Pak nuclear collaboration began in 1971. China has a long history of providing nuclear and missile-related assistance to Pakistan, including weapons-grade uranium and warhead designs, with the majority of its assistance occurring in the 1980s and 1990s. Analysts generally interpret Beijing's motivation for assisting Pakistan as being rooted in its objective of containing India's regional power aspirations. Pakistan Prime Minister Bhutto had once remarked in the aftermath of the Indian nuclear test that "If India builds the bomb, we will eat grass or leaves, even go hungry, but we will get one of our own." Reports reveal that 1976 was the inaugural year for China-Pakistan nuclear collaboration, with American concerns about this cooperation following suit. Talks between US Secretary of State Henry Kissinger and Bhutto during this period, discussed the nuclear cooperation between the two countries, however, the focus was on nuclear reprocessing and uranium enrichment was not yet a concern. In 1986, a formal treaty out lining the nuclear cooperation between China and Pakistan was signed. 1986 is also significant, since it came at the height of the Cold War conflict in Afghanistan, and therefore, an ideological battle for influence in the region was being fought by the two super powers. Pakistan recognized its frontline role in being the vanguard for the Islamic world against Communism, following which President Zia ul Haq rhetorically declared the following about nuclear weapons: "It is our right to obtain technology and when we acquire this technology the Islamic world will possess it with us."

The 1986 treaty, as mentioned above, was the formalization of a robust nuclear transfer which was already underway between the two countries. According to Dr AQ Khan, father of Pakistan's nuclear program, serious nuclear cooperation between Pakistan and China is documented as early as 1982. He has cited the case of a Pakistani military C-130 which left the Chinese city of Urumqi with enough weapons-grade uranium for two atomic bombs. The yield for these weapons is estimated at 20-25KT. Additional transfers included blueprints to develop the nuclear weapons.

Cooperation between the two countries steadily increased in the following years, with substantial transfers occurring in the decade of 1986-1996. According to media reports, during this period , in addition to assisting with the Kahuta nuclear reactor, the Chinese also transferred tritium gas, which is used in the manufacture of a hydrogen bomb. Beijing also supplied heavy water (D_2O) to the safeguarded Kanupp reactor (originally supplied by Canada) at a rate to make up heavy-water losses of 2 to 4 per cent a year. It is also believed that China offered its test facilities at Lop Nor in 1989, to conduct a Pakistani nuclear test. While the international community was increasingly aware of such transactions, the response to them was limited owing to a variety of geo-strategic and diplomatic considerations. One of them was economic; in 1985 the Chinese and US governments signed a Nuclear Cooperation Agreement (NCA) that, when enacted, would allowed the American firms to apply for licenses to sell nuclear reactors to China. Implementing the agreement on the US side required the US President to certify to the Congress that China was not proliferating nuclear weapons. Additionally, the Pressler Amendment was passed which required the US government to certify at the start of each fiscal year, that Pakistan did not possess a nuclear device. The US government did so, since Pakistan was a frontline ally, against the Soviets in Afghanistan.

On 30 May 1989, American questioned Chinese over their cooperation with Pakistan which the Chinese denied and stated that Beijing's accession to the IAEA in 1984 required all its transactions to be conducted under safeguards. It was largely owing to Chinese efforts that Pakistan was nuclear weapons capable by 1989 itself. A partial admission was provided by Former Pakistan Prime Minister Benazir Bhutto when she admitted that a cold test had been conducted in 1989. Despite international scrutiny, in 1991, China agreed to build the Chashma 300-MW nuclear power reactor for Pakistan. In order to lend international credibility to this exercise, Pakistan was asked to sign an IAEA safeguards (limited-scope) agreement for the reactor at Chashma. Significantly, while these proliferation rings were being strengthened, China was not a part of the Nuclear Non-Proliferation Treaty, and therefore not violating its principles. China signed the Nuclear Nonproliferation Treaty in 1992 and the Comprehensive Test Ban Treaty in 1995. China's tactics to violate its international obligations were evident during the immediate period after the end of the Cold War, with Chinese firms acting as fronts for transferring European technology to Pakistan. These firms attempted to buy German cooling equipment for reactors to supply Pakistan, for use in its Chasma reactors. Similarly, further attempts at proliferation were seen in 1995, when 5,000 specially designed ring magnets from the China Nuclear Energy Industry Corporation (CNEIC), were sold to an un-safeguarded Pakistani nuclear facility. When questioned by the US, China initially denied any such transfers. Later China admitted to the fact but argued that the ring magnets were not magnetized, and the Nuclear Suppliers Group (NSG) Trigger List only covered ring magnets magnetized at a specific tolerance.

As per the CIA, China was the primary source of nuclear-related equipment and technology to Pakistan, during the second half of 1996. This cooperation continued into the late 1990s, culminating with alleged assistance to Pakistan in its immediate response to the Indian nuclear test of 1998. United States itself took over two weeks to retaliate to a Soviet nuclear test, despite having the weapon for years. Therefore, the Pakistani device was a pre-engineered one, which their scientists had great confidence in. Chinese proliferation has not seen periods of low activity even during periods of tumultuous developments in the region, including the Kargil Conflict of 1999, during which China maintained a neutral position.

In 2005 discussions on the Indo-US nuclear agreement began which resulted in China taking an active interest in the regional implications for its strategic partner, and opposed the agreement on grounds that it is not equitable, and favoured a similar NSG exemption for Pakistan. When the international community expressed its reservations on Pakistan's non-proliferation record (based on inputs that Dr. Khan had further proliferated Chinese designs to Libya, North Korea and Iran), China took it upon itself to strengthen its nuclear relationship with Pakistan.

As per Nuclear Threat Initiative, in September 2010 China announced its intention to sell two additional plutonium-producing heavy water reactors to Pakistan. For several years, Pakistan's nuclear program has been a source of concern for the international community, due to the country's past involvement in illicit proliferation and the persistent terrorist violence and instability plaguing Pakistan. This nuclear deal with China adds another complicating factor into analysis of the state of Islamabad's nuclear program. It seems clear that China's motivations in undertaking the deal relate less to the likely impact on Islamabad's nuclear program, and more to Beijing's regional balance of power and strategic stability priorities.

At present, Pakistan has between 90 and 100 nuclear weapons, and is steadily expanding its nuclear weapons program through newer installations at facilities such as the Khushab complex. The Khushab complex contains a 40 to 50 MW heavy water plutonium production reactor, as well as two other heavy water reactors under construction. The construction of these reactors and the expansion of reprocessing facilities suggest that Islamabad is focusing on refining its nuclear weapons arsenal. The two reactors under the latest agreement will be based at the Chashma nuclear complex in Punjab province, where China is already constructing two other reactors from an earlier bilateral deal. According to Pakistani officials, Beijing is offering extremely generous financial conditions, without which the deal would have been a non-starter for Islamabad. The first reactor at the Chashma complex, a 325MW plant called Chashma-I, is based on a 1991 agreement between China and Pakistan. According China, the latest expansion project at Chashma is part of a 2003 agreement between Islamabad and Beijing. When China joined the Nuclear Suppliers Group (NSG) in 2004 it informed NSG member states that apart from Chashma 1 and 2 it would not supply any further reactors to Pakistan. Beijing also listed the items it was committed to export to Islamabad under the original agreement. The NSG issue is crucial since under the group's rules, nuclear fuel, reactors, and technology cannot be supplied to countries, such as Pakistan, who do not adopt full-scope safeguards. Beijing is seeking to "grandfather" the two-reactor deal through the 2003 agreement, since this agreement was concluded before China's entry into the NSG. In addition to the two new reactors for the Chashma complex, the China National Nuclear Corporation (CNNC) will supply a fifth nuclear reactor to Pakistan with a 1GW capacity. But there is no indication that this reactor deal, which presumably will not be part of the Chashma complex, was approved by or even brought before the NSG. According to one account, at the 2010 NSG plenary meeting, even though several member states had requested clarifications from China regarding the deal, Beijing responded that all exports to Pakistan would follow NSG guidelines, implying that the latest round of reactor transactions would be grandfathered through the earlier 2003 agreement. The Pakistani position is that the deal does not violate its non proliferation obligations, because it is not connected to the military side of its nuclear program.

Islamabad has also stated that the proposed reactors at Chashma are crucial to its efforts to generate 8,800MW of nuclear energy by 2030. Although Pakistan does have a major energy shortfall, these older generation reactors that comprise Chashma 3 and 4 will do little to address the problem – when they do become operational at least six years from now, the reactors will cover only 20 percent of the deficit.

Islamabad has also expressed an interest in joining the NSG and other export control regimes (the Missile Technology Control Regime, and the Wassenaar and Australia Groups). This comes close on the heels of India's push to join the NSG, which was endorsed by the Obama administration in late 2010. Indeed, in recent years, Pakistan's objections to the current Fissile Material Cutoff Treaty (FMCT) proposals have revolved around its position that the Indo-U.S. nuclear deal upsets the balance in South Asia. As U.S. Secretary of State Hillary Clinton said at a Congressional committee hearing, for Islamabad, ties between India and the United States are a "zero-sum game," meaning that any major initiative between the two sides has a negative impact on U.S.-Pakistan relations, and by extension, Pakistan's position in South Asia.

This highlights two related themes governing Pakistani nuclear and overall foreign policy making: (1) that it is reactive to India's policies on nuclear matters; and (2) that Islamabad is convinced of the need to appear as India's equal in the nuclear realm and is being assisted by China to achieve this parity. Pakistan's opinion is that it should be accorded any benefits or concessions that India has received from the international community. Some analysts have speculated that Islamabad's demands for a nuclear deal from the United States might be a bargaining tactic for benefits in other areas, especially economic and conventional military aid. It is not clear if Islamabad would be willing to accept intrusive oversight of its nuclear facilities, which would be the price of a nuclear deal with Washington, especially at a time when domestic audiences in Pakistan are suspicious of Washington's intentions regarding Pakistan's nuclear program. Therefore, Pakistan might prefer to seek nuclear assistance from Beijing, who is unlikely to demand such oversight.

For China, the deal with Pakistan is a way of providing some compensatory benefits to a key ally at a time when Islamabad has been under persistent international pressure in the context of the campaign against Al-Qaeda and the Taliban in the region. However, given that Beijing did not press for an across-the-board NSG exemption for Pakistan, this deal is limited in its scope. It is, therefore, an attempt to restore some semblance of balance of power in South Asia and assuage a key ally. Beijing might also be concerned about expanding ties between New Delhi and Washington and India's quest for a higher global role and status. Thus, the need to balance India's ties not just with the United States but also with other Asian powers like Japan is likely to have been a factor behind the deal with Pakistan. By allowing Islamabad to reinforce its strategic ties with Beijing at a time of added U.S. pressure on Pakistan, China seeks to check Indian and American geo-strategic positioning in the region. Additionally, Beijing is also seeking to be an important player in international nuclear commerce and the deals with Pakistan help demonstrate its increasing role in this regard.

Nevertheless, China seems to have pursued the Sino-Pakistani deal with caution. There is no adequate information in the public domain regarding the Sino-Pakistani negotiating process in the years prior to the official announcement of the deal in 2010. Both China and Pakistan waited while the Indo-U.S. nuclear agreement went through the various stages of the negotiating process to see whether the deal would actually be approved by the NSG, the IAEA and the Indian and U.S. legislatures. Although Islamabad was in favor of finalizing its own deal in 2006, Beijing preferred to see if the Indo-U.S. agreement fulfilled all procedural steps, including getting the NSG exemption. An alleged U.S. diplomatic cable from 2006 which was released by Wikileaks backs the view that the Sino-Pakistani deal is a response to the Indo-U.S. deal. In the cable, a Chinese foreign ministry official is quoted as reassuring a U.S. interlocutor that reports of an agreement to supply two reactors to Pakistan were baseless and that as an NSG member, Beijing would abide by its international obligations. The ultimate passage of the Indo-U.S. agreement in 2008 can help explain why China reversed this position. It was only after the Indo-U.S. deal was approved and New Delhi re-entered international nuclear trade that the Sino-Pakistani deal was announced. In fact, Chinese officials have justified their deal with Pakistan by citing the Indo-U.S. nuclear deal.

But the Sino-Pakistani deal is different from the Indo-U.S. agreement. In the Indian case, the agreement went through the various procedural steps, whether at the IAEA, the NSG or the legislatures of the United States and India, and only then was it implemented through specific deals with various suppliers. In the Sino-Pakistani case, the parties did not seek formal approval from the NSG, and China preferred to "grandfather" the reactor transaction despite earlier commitments to desist from doing so. Moreover, attempts by China and Pakistan to conclude a nuclear deal that would add to the Chashma 1 and 2 reactors predate the Indo-U.S. nuclear agreement by several years; preparations for this deal were already made when the Indo-US deal was announced. Therefore, it may not be completely accurate to suggest that the Sino-Pakistani deal was a direct result of the Indo-U.S. deal.

Nuclear matters concerning Pakistan have been a source of unease for the international community. The expansion of terrorist violence in Pakistan has raised the international concerns about the security of the country's nuclear weapons, materials, and facilities. Despite these concerns, so far the international community has accepted the Sino – Pak deal as a fait accompli and despite some dissatisfaction with the deal, has not opposed its progress. In March 2011, the International Atomic Energy Agency (IAEA) approved a safeguards agreement with Pakistan for the Chashma 3 & 4 reactors, with no objections from any IAEA board members. The U.S has tried to balance various competing regional and global priorities. In March 2011, U.S. Assistant Secretary of State, Robert Blake informed that the USA expected China to abide by the commitments that it made when it joined the Nuclear Suppliers Group in 2004, and the construction of new nuclear reactors - Chashma 3 and 4 would be inconsistent with these commitments. Thus, despite the deal being inconsistent with China's NSG obligations, the U.S. did not oppose it on the grounds that it is important for Pakistan's energy requirements. It is likely that the need to maintain Pakistan's support in the campaign against the Taliban and Al Qaeda has played a bigger role in Washington's acquiescence to the deal. Other important objectives might also have affected Washington's capacity to pressure China to desist from proceeding with the agreement, especially the need for Beijing's support for tougher sanctions against Iran.

India on its part appears to also essentially submitted to the deal and has not expressed any public opposition to it. India did, however, ask Beijing for clarity and transparency on the deal. According to Indian analyses, the reactor deal does not significantly strengthen Islamabad's nuclear arsenal, mainly because the facilities would be under safeguards. Moreover, the key determinant of Islamabad's nuclear weapons program is not the Chashma complex, but rather the capacity of the Kahuta enrichment facility, the heavy water reactor at Khushab, and Pakistan's uranium stock. This reinforces the notion that Islamabad's insistence on a civilian nuclear agreement is, in large part, an attempt to maintain some degree of geopolitical parity with India, which is being supported by China.

As per a report published by Salman Masood and Chris Buckley on November 26, 2013 (available on the internet), Pakistan has been able to achieve a deal with China to build a nuclear power complex in Karachi for $9.59 billion, seeking to ease Pakistan's long-running energy crisis and signaling a new step by China in becoming a top nuclear supplier. The deal, which officials said was still being finalized, is a major new advance in energy cooperation between the two countries, dwarfing previous reactor projects built along with China at Chashma, in Pakistan's interior and it establishes a growing counterpoint to a nuclear axis between the United States and India in recent years that Pakistani officials have seen as an irritant and Chinese officials have seen as a geopolitical challenge. As per the report, the new project is to be built around two new-model Chinese ACP-1000 nuclear reactors, with China also providing enriched uranium for fuel. China has also signaled its intent to expand nuclear energy cooperation with Pakistan.

The Sino-Pak nuclear collaboration will continue to be driven primarily by balance of power considerations, as well as issue linkages with other pressing matters. From the Pakistani perspective, it is an opportunity for closing the gap with India on nuclear matters and reversing the "de-hyphenation" with its South Asian neighbor. The matter is likely to gain more impetus with the recent Indo – US nuclear deal. For China the deal is about balance of power issues.

Beijing is trying to ensure that India's profile is restricted to South Asia by bolstering Pakistan and countering increased U.S. influence in the region. The collaboration also raises questions about the capacity of the Nuclear Suppliers Group and its ability to prevent such collaboration.

4 | SINO – PAK SPACE COLLABORATION

Over the years Pakistan has shown a copycat syndrome with reference to India as far as strategically important programmes are concerned. Since Pakistan's technological and industrial base is not well-established, it has relied on foreign assistance. Initially Pakistan's investments in space technologies were minimal. This is surprising because it has a reasonably well-developed Chinese assisted missile programme which, in fact, could have helped at least partially to build up an indigenous space programme. Pakistan's lack of interest in space technology is primarily due to three reasons. Firstly, Pakistan's focus on long-term investments in technology has predominantly been military in nature. The use of technology for social, educational and scientific needs was not the prime focus. Secondly, Pakistan appears to have failed to anticipate the long-term strategic importance of space technology in spite of its nuclear ambitions. Thirdly, because of superfluous investments in military hardware, Pakistan was unable to make investments in space technology and also it appears to have failed to realize the future commercial relevance of a space programme. On the other hand China has been confident of its space capability and has wanted to employ this to gain strategic influence in the world. The advent of Chinese commercial space-launch services goes back to 1986 and as usual Pakistan was a beneficiary of this commercial expansion.

India's forays into space compelled Pakistan to follow suit. In view of Pakistan's limitations in developing an independent space programme, the only option it had was to seek China's assistance. China was responsible for launching Pakistan's first indigenously made satellite Badr-1 in 1990. The operation of this satellite gave

Pakistani scientists a practical understanding of telemetry, orbital patterns, surveillance and Chinese launch platforms. In 1991, an agreement was formalized between China and Pakistan on the space cooperation. Post-1991, space technologies did not feature very high on Pakistan's set of priorities. It was only recently that a surge has been observed in space-related co-operation between China and Pakistan. It was after more than two decades of the 1990 launch that Sino-Pak space cooperation saw another landmark event, when China launched Pakistan's communication satellite, PAKSAT-1R from its Satellite Launch Center in Sichuan Province. This launch took place in August 2011. The launch marked China's first "in-orbit delivery" for an Asian country. The deal to develop the satellite was concluded in 2008 and Pakistan received a loan of RMB 222 million (US$34.7 million). An additional concessional loan of RMB 86.5 million (US$13.5 million) was given to Pakistan in 2010 by the EXIM Bank of China.

China has been responsible for establishing a substantial level of aerospace infrastructure in Pakistan. Working alongside the Chinese scientists, the Pakistani scientists have gained hands-on experience, which would be helpful for future assignments and indigenization. PAKSAT-1R has replaced the old PAKSAT-1 and would provide TV broadcasting, internet access, data communication services, disaster warning etc. and help boost Pakistan's economy. Pakistan Army is one of the 45 clients of PAKSAT-1R and the satellite is expected to provide strategic military and cross-border applications. China's collaboration will help Pakistan defence forces in enhancing their combat capabilities and transform its war fighting strategies.

In 2006, China agreed to facilitate launch of three earth resource satellites stretching over five years. In 2009, the two countries signed an agreement to promote satellite technology worth $222 million. According to the agreement, the various projects under PAKSAT-II would be accomplished by utilizing the easy loan provided by China for 20 years. The agreement also stipulated that PAKSAT II, III and IV would be completed by using technology from China and Turkey. During the visit of Pakistani PM to China in 2011, it was agreed that a working group would be formed to conduct negotiations for the purchase of satellites from China. This comes amidst reports that Chinese state-owned firms are keen to tap the international market especially in the developing countries. China has been known to transfer sensitive technologies as a part of its geopolitical strategy when dealing with developing countries. Pakistan's growing international isolation, financial constraints combined with western opposition disallows it to earn generous partnerships in high-end technologies with other players in the domain. On the other hand, Chinese state-owned companies render monetary privileges in the form of loans and competitive quotes. The support of the Chinese government to state companies gives it an edge in international competition, unlike foreign corporations which finalise deals based on profitability and in accordance with their governmental laws.

As a result of the above, Pakistan treasures its friendship with the Chinese for it is the only country capable and willing to help it in space technology and for China the space cooperation is yet another way to expand its space frontiers and showcase itself as a leader of third world countries which follows non-discriminatory international practices. Space diplomacy has been extensively employed by China to engage with countries in Africa and Latin American in lieu of access to their natural recourses like oil, minerals etc. Other countries like Pakistan, Bolivia, Nigeria and Venezuela have in the recent past gauged the importance of space technology are being supported by China. Apart from commercial interests, Beijing's geopolitical interests are deeply embedded in its cooperation, instantly earning it a degree of influence in the client states. Militarily, China does not expect any major benefit from Pakistan in space cooperation because of its dependence on China and lack of sophisticated technology. China's focus is primarily on economic expansion, showcasing soft power, gaining access to resources or geographical locations and posing as an attractive entrepreneur in the global market.

China's policy of supporting Pakistan to counter balance India is once again manifested in China's space relations with Pakistan. As Beijing's space programme advances forward, Pakistan becomes an important beneficiary. Pakistan has also benefitted immensely from various space projects launched by China such as the BeiDou (Compass) Navigation System which is a satellite navigation system consisting of 35 satellites and seeks to replace its reliance on US Global Positioning System (GPS). The project is currently under development and is scheduled to be completed by 2020. The project would assist in mapping, fishery, transport, meteorology and telecommunications. Military applications would include navigation and munitions guidance and obviate its dependence on a foreign system. Pakistan has shown interest in the project and technical negotiations are under progress. Pakistan's armed forces would benefit greatly from Bei Dou by gaining access to a secure navigational system and defence-grade satellite imaging, thus gaining a strategic edge in the region.

Pakistan has also sought China's participation in the development of Pakistan Remote Sensing Satellite (PRSS), which forms a part of National Satellite Development Program. High resolution PRSS is a dual-purpose earth observational and optical satellite and is scheduled for launch in 2014. Apart from civilian application, the satellite would also be used for military purposes. Once established, PRSS would definitely transform into an indispensable part of Pakistan's military activities. PRSS will give Pakistan's armed forces an accurate system for reconnaissance and surveillance of the adversary's zones of interest, strategic sites, troop deployment, geographical weaknesses and strengths. The system can also be employed for navigation, target tracking, bomb and missile guidance thereby enhancing lethality, rescue, facility management and for constantly updating maps.

The implications of Sino-Pak space collaboration impinges on India's strategic concerns in South Asia and its national security. Chinese's assistance to Pakistan has given a boost to latter's defence forces and space-based cooperation would provide them with more precision during future warfare operations against India. Experts feel that in case of an Indo-Pak conflict, China's space assets would prove advantageous for Pakistan's defence forces. Given PLA's proximity to

Pakistan's forces, access to China's aerospace information systems and sharing of critical data is most likely. More importantly, China plans to help Pakistan to a level where it can independently tackle India and undertake space-based operations. Such a policy gives PLA the breathing space to not get pulled into Pakistan's war against India. Chinese space assets would enhance Pakistan's air power and naval operations, in terms of surveillance, communications, navigation and providing support for manned flights etc. Chinese support would be essential to match up to India's capabilities. Sino-Pakistan space cooperation is bound to expand and it would be imperative for India to factor in Pakistan and China's space capabilities and their future projects, which could impinge upon its national security. India needs to look at these developments seriously and needs to factor these in its strategic planning.

5 | ECONOMIC COOPERATION

Historically, trade between the two countries dates back almost 3000 years when Pakistan was a part of undivided India. Trade was carried out along the silk route which was closed in 1949 and was reopened in 1967. The economic interaction between China and Pakistan began in 1950s. The first trade agreement was signed in 1963. In 1982 the two countries established Pakistan-China Joint Committee on Economy, Trade and Technology. Trade between China and Pakistan has been generally conducted under 1963 Trade Agreement, according to which, both countries have granted MFN status to each other.

Despite the multi -modal trade i.e. barter trade and cash trade between the two countries, the trade balance has always titled in favour of China. China, on its part has tried to compensate the trade deficit by providing generous assistance to Pakistan to build infrastructure and acquire self-sufficiency. Most part of this assistance was either grants or interest-free loan. Pakistan has undertaken several major projects with the Chinese help which include Karakoram Highway (KKH), Gwadar Deep Seaport, Chasma Nuclear Power Plant, Indus Highway, Thar Coal Development, Saindak Metal Project, Makran Coastal Highway, power generation projects, both nuclear and non-nuclear and oil pipelines. In addition to the public sector, China has also invested in Pakistani private sector.

In 2004, the two countries signed seven agreements in trade, communication and energy sector and drew up a framework for greater cooperation. These agreements proved a step forward towards increase in bilateral trade, further movement on preferential trade agreement, setting up of joint agro-based industries and increased Chinese investment in Pakistan. Pakistan announced Free Market Economy (FME) status for China. In recent years, China has taken several steps and initiatives to improve its trade and investment relations with Pakistan. 2006 saw the signing of the bilateral Free Trade Agreement (FTA) and the five year Development Program on Economic and Trade Cooperation - directed at accelerating bilateral trade between Pakistan and China. It set a trade target of $15b by 2010 while this target was not achieved, bilateral trade - that stood at $7b in 2006 - rose to$12b by 2012. In 2006 China was Pakistan's third largest trading partner, accounting for 9.8 percent of Pakistan's imports. It ranked 11th (3 percent) for Pakistan's exports. In comparison, Pakistan was China's 54th largest trading partner (0.13 percent of China's imports) and 33rd largest for exports (0.44 percent). By 2013, China was Pakistan's second largest trading partner. From 2004-2008 exports from China to Pakistan have increased on average 55 percent per annum while exports from Pakistan to China rose by 35 percent. The Development Program was renewed in late 2010 and included 36 different projects covering education, health care, energy, water, environment and information and communications technology. Presently, Pakistan is the only country in South Asia with a free trade agreement and currency swap agreement with China. To stimulate the trade growth, in May 2013, State Bank of Pakistan and People's Bank of China agreed on a currency swap arrangement implying that the two countries can now trade directly without the use of US dollars as the intermediary trade currency. However, the trade imbalance is one of Pakistan's main concerns and measures to lessen the gap are frequently discussed and calculated efforts are being made to raise export levels to China. To bring economic cooperation at par with political and defence cooperation is now on the front burner Islamabad's policy towards China. It is in Chinese interests too, to strengthen economic ties with Pakistan.

As per news reports on 08 Nov 2014, during the Asia Pacific Economic Cooperation (APEC) organised by China, the two countries have signed 20 agreements amounting to Chinese investment reportedly worth about $46 billion to further boost the bilateral ties in various fields, including energy and basic infrastructure sectors. The agreements signed between the two countries include solar power production Quaid-e Azam Solar Park, easy loan for laying optic fibre between the two countries, mining of 65,00,000 metric tons of coal in Thar Block-2, 870 MW Sukhi Kinari hydropower project, 1320 MW Sahiwal power project and MoU for 100 MW Jhimpir wind power project. An agreement has also been signed to establish an Industrial Park in Faisalabad, Pakistan. The two countries have also inked an agreement for economic and technical cooperation. They have also expressed their resolve to materialise the much publicised multi-billion dollar China-Pakistan Economic Corridor connecting western China to Gwadar Port in Pakistan. According to some experts, Gwadar Port presents an opportunity to China as it stands to save a lot by rerouting trade from Urumqi to Gwadar. The route to the Persian Gulf is 2,500km long, as opposed to the currently used eastern sea route that is 10,000km and where tankers are vulnerable to naval blockade in case of war. Gwadar route offers a safer and a shorter alternative to China. Gwadar is often termed a "game-changer" in Pakistan. Both countries are committed to the economic corridor that is likely to materialise in few years. While China needs the alternative route from an economic and energy perspective, Pakistan needs the opportunities and cash generated by Gwadar port. However, the ground realities indicate the geographical and political difficulties which are likely to be encountered which developing the corridor.

Appraisal Sino – Pak Economic Corridor

China has established cordial relations, economic and strategic partnerships with most of its neighbours which allow it to obtain its energy requirements to sustain its economic growth and extend its influence. It has been following a strategy of trade, security access and basing facilities in South East Asia, Indian Ocean and areas in proximity to oil rich Gulf region.

China's hydrocarbon utilization has doubled in past two decades and will continue to rise. It is the world's second largest oil consumer and the largest oil importer. Oil consumption is expected to grow in China by 5.8 percent annually until 2015. Oil imported from the Gulf States and Africa comprises 70 percent of total Chinese oil imports, and remains China's most critical source of energy apart from domestic coal production. Chinese analysts estimate that China would need six hundred million tons of oil a year from 2020 onwards and it would end up importing more than 70 per cent of its oil requirement. Presently China is importing majority of its oil through the Indian Ocean and the Strait of Malacca. In the event of a conflict, these routes could be interdicted, choking China's energy supply especially at the Malacca Strait. Chinese leadership has been trying to mitigate this 'Malacca Dilemma' by reinforcing its naval presence in the Indian Ocean and developing overland trade and energy corridors. One such effort has been the much hyped economic corridor with Pakistan. The two countries signed eight Memorandums of Understanding (MoU) and Agreements to strengthen economic and diplomatic ties. One of the important agreements includes an economic corridor, to be built at the cost of US$ 18 billion, which will link Pakistan's Gwadar Port on the Arabian Sea and Kashghar in Xinjiang in northwest China. Under the project, Beijing is expected to add a railway line, fibre optic link and a petroleum pipeline across the Karakoram. It would also involve the development of industrial projects along the Corridor and construction of a massive special economic zone in Gwadar. According to Pakistan, the Economic Corridor is a 'game changer' for the whole region. No doubt that this economic corridor, if it materializes, will be of immense benefit to both China and Pakistan. This appraisal attempts to analyse the ground realities related to various facets of the corridor.

Gwadar Deep Sea Port

Gwadar Port is the third deep sea port in Pakistan after Karachi and Port Qasim. Located on the western end of Baluchistan coast, Gwadar has a 600 km long coastal belt. It lies 624 nautical km to the east of Strait of Hormuz, which is an important route of oil tankers bound for Asian economies and western countries out of the Persian Gulf. In 2007 Pakistan handed over the port operations to Port of Singapore Authority (PSA) for 25 years. PSA withdrew after Islamabad refused to provide large land allotments which the PSA wanted for development work around the port.

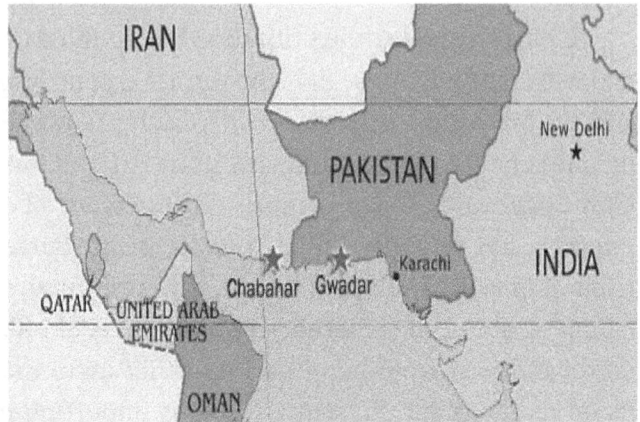

Gwadar Port has great strategic value, enhancing Pakistan's importance in the whole region as it is close to the Strait of Hormuz, through which more than 13 million barrel oil per day passes. It offers a prime location to monitor shipping passing through the Strait of Hormuz from the Persian Gulf, as well as access to cheap land routes or Middle East trade through Pakistan into western China and Central Asia. In February 2013, Pakistan government transferred the operational control of Gwadar to China. The Port offers a shorter route to western China—via the recently expanded Karakoram highway across Gilgit-Baltistan in northern Pakistan—and an alternative route to vulnerable sea lanes through the Strait of Malacca. Iran had also announced its intention to set up an oil refinery with oil production capacity of 400,000 barrels per day at Gwadar Port. Besides, as an alternative deep water port, it is situated 470 km away from Karachi making it less vulnerable to Indian naval blockade which Pakistan faced in 1971 war. Due to its strategic location and because the strong military ties between China and Pakistan, Gwadar port has received excessive attention from the very beginning.

Gwadar is located in politically volatile Baluchistan Province, which has poor infrastructure. Gwadar and its surrounding areas lack any significant infrastructure. The port needs to be connected to Pakistan's national road network. Importing and exporting via Gwadar would therefore be difficult and costly, which could cause the port to fall into significant financial difficulty. Moves to assuage these problems include connectivity to the highways, establishing free economic zones and making Gwadar a free port on lines of Hong Kong or Singapore. These developments are presently progressing slowly.

Another threat to the port is from the insurgents in Baluchistan. These groups are fighting the Pakistani military and demanding autonomy. Some have appealed to USA for support and have opposed China's building of the port at Gwadar. The main threat comes from the Baluchistan Liberation Army (BLA), which seeks to have Baluchistan secede from Pakistan citing Islamabad's exploitation of the region's people and resources. The BLA has condemned building of the port as a conspiracy to rob the Baluchi people. Some Chinese workers in the past have been victims of targeted attacks. The serious view of the threat taken by the Pakistan Government can be seen in the increasing security measures around the port. Though China has built some roads in Pakistan, it still needs to lay thousands of kilometers of gas and oil pipelines and railway track in order to turn Gwadar for economic use. China is reluctant to invest in this volatile region. A number of feudal lords are opposed to large-scale foreign investment, fearing that it would bring an influx of outsiders. They demand greater autonomy and royalties for the extraction of natural resources. Although China has developed local infrastructure, it is considered an 'exploiter'. The port has failed to draw any major business since its completion in 2006. The fact that the port remained unused was one reason the PSA withdrew. Unlike Islamabad's tall claims about the port's geo-economic significance, China has taken a more cautious and realistic approach. China appears to be doubtful of the port's profitability. Pakistan had to drag China in 2001 to finance the first phase of the port and in 2013 to take over administrative control of the port. Despite its being over a decade since China started construction of the first phase, no PLA related activity has been observed in the area. If China had intended to use a Pakistani port for naval purposes then Karachi with its established military infrastructure, is an available alternative although it has the strategic disadvantage of proximity to India.

In the present scenario China will develop the port quickly by making a bigger investment than the PSA, but its current interests appear commercial, aimed at securing its energy supplies. Moreover, Gwadar is just one of several options for Beijing, and due to the volatile security situation in the surrounding region it may not be China's best bet. Gwadar is far from becoming a Chinese economic hub, let alone a security asset. Gwadar is not the only option for the Chinese in the Indian Ocean. It is not even the most viable option. Beijing has developed Hambantota and Colombo ports in Sri Lanka and a container facility in Chittagong. In Myanmar, China has built roads, dams and oil and gas pipelines.

Road Link

In order to make Gwadar port as an economic base, China would have to deal with the problems plaguing the Karakoram Highway

(KKH) which passes through some of the most inhospitable terrain in the world. The success of Gwadar as a Chinese trading post depends upon the stability of the 1,300-kilometer KKH which is China's only overland link to Pakistan. Without the KKH there is no land route to Gwadar. Without a reliable land route to the port, Gwadar's value decreases drastically and the KKH is anything but reliable. China has already begun upgrading the Karakoram Highway that runs through the north western Xinjiang region to the border with Pakistan and has commenced developmental projects high in the mountains of the Pakistan occupied Kashmir.

The geographical and security challenges to the highway remain formidable. It would go through a territory threatened by the Pakistani Taliban, while nationalists in Baluchistan view it as an attempt by the Punjabis to strengthen their control over the desert region and plunder its natural resources. Pakistan and China have signed an eight memoranda of understanding agreements with an eye toward accelerating economic integration between the two countries. Among these was a pact to develop an economic corridor from Kashgar to Gwadar. One of the agreements includes construction of 200 km-long tunnel that amounts to $18 billion in cost. The proposed alignment will include more than 100 tunnels with a total length of 200 km; majority will be less than 5 km length. The longest tunnel would be approximately 24 km at Mintaka Pass near Pak – China border. As per Pakistan this would facilitate move of traffic throughout the year.

The pact also includes establishment of a joint committee to oversee the upgrade and realignment of the KKH, which is desperately in need of improvement. Expansion of the KKH is a challenging prospect, even for China's experienced road builders. Since 1970s inspite of joint efforts by both the countries the highway has remained sealed in some sections, unsealed in others, with Pakistani and Chinese workers improving the most hazardous bits in piecemeal fashion over the years. During wintertime, the Khunjerab Pass to China closes due to heavy snow. KKH winds through an earthquake prone area. The region is webbed with fault lines, making frequent seismic activities. The epicentre of Kashmir earthquake in 2005 was located less than 10 km from the highway resulting in destruction of infrastructure and blocked parts of the highway for weeks. Landslides are also a common occurrence and the road is regularly blocked by boulders and rubble. Since much of the KKH is narrow, even a small landslide can immobilize traffic in both directions until the debris is cleared. The area is also prone to floods and the glacial runoff during the summer destroys bridges, stranding traffic occasionally for more than a month at a time.

The proposed link would be passing close to the disputed Pak-Afghan border especially near the Wakhan Corridor. The link may be vulnerable to additional security threats in case an anti–Pakistan government comes to power in Afghanistan after withdrawal of ISAF.

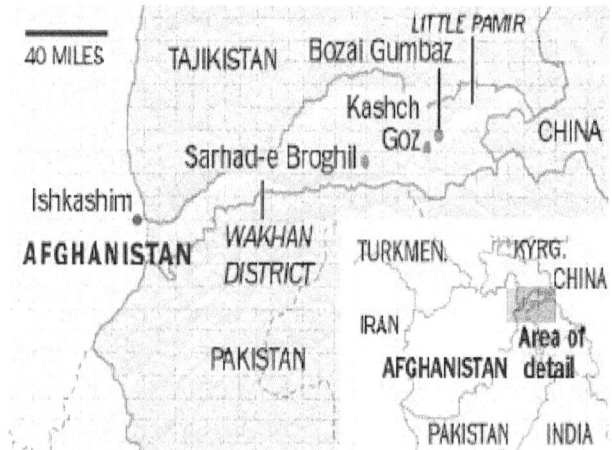

Railway Link

The proposed rail link to boost economic relations between China and Pakistan also faces the same problem as the road and oil pipeline projects. The rail link would be required to be laid in an area having difficult terrain, insurgent activity, frequent avalanches, landslides and seismic activity. Such a project would require high construction and transportation costs. The tariffs needed to pay off the finance costs of the route and move of freight over a 15,000 foot vertical relief would likely make the cost highly uncompetitive as compared to sea route. The 2,000 km-long Qingzang railway link to Lhasa cost approximately US$4 billion to build which translates to US$1.85 million per km. The cost per km to build a rail line connecting Islamabad and Kashgar could be several times more expensive to build.

The availability of construction area would restrict laying of one track each way which will reduce the load carriage capacity. Trains moving through the Khunjerab Pass would carry smaller loads, perhaps 2,000 tons, due to the large vertical gradient. With these train frequency and load parameters, the corridor would be able to handle 8.75 million tons of cargo per year, or approximately 175,000 barrels of oil per day if all the trains carried oil. To move the volumes that would be necessary to make this route be able to handle enough cargo to reduce reliance on sea route it would need a rail network with at least 3 to 4 lines. Furthermore, bringing that much cargo into China's Western rail network and then having to move it into industrial areas in the central and eastern regions would require additional capacity expansions of the national rail system. These investments would likely be cost-prohibitive.

Pakistan–China Oil Pipeline

Another ambitious project is to lay oil pipeline from Pakistan to western China to diversify China's oil import routes and avoid the Malacca Strait. Iran has also expressed its willingness to become a part of this pipeline network. However, it is assessed that geographic and security problems render such an oil pipeline unfeasible in the near and medium terms. Chinese have expressed grave reservations about the security situation in Pakistan in light of the country's perpetual violence and increasing political instability, along with the rise of Islamic fundamentalism and terrorist attacks against outsiders. Chinese workers have been kidnapped and killed in western and north western Pakistan, the regions that would be traversed by the oil pipeline. The pipeline would also transit a part of POK, proximity of which to India would lend itself to disruption in case of a war between India and Pakistan.

In addition to security problems, there would also be serious financial barriers, since oil transport costs could run to at least ten dollars a barrel to achieve payout plus a 10 percent rate of return. Even at a price above a hundred dollars a barrel, a transport cost of nine to ten dollars a barrel is very high compared to that of seaborne shipping. The cost disparity between maritime and pipeline shipping would be greater as it could cost up to 10 dollars to move a barrel of oil to Urumqi in western China. After reaching Urumqi, the oil would have to be piped an additional three or four thousand km to reach major east coast demand centres, meaning that transport costs from the Persian Gulf to Chinese end users could exceed fifteen dollars a barrel, as opposed to closer to US$2.00/barrel for oil transported from the Gulf to eastern China on super tankers. This venture may prove uneconomical for China.

Geography, construction and maintenance cost would pose major challenges to the proposed pipeline. The pipeline would have to be constructed in some of the world's most challenging terrain. Moreover, it would need to lift oil from sea level at Gwadar up to the 15,500 foot-high Khunjerab Pass, requiring massive pumping power and steady electrical supplies in remote areas vulnerable to insurgent activity. By way of comparison, the Trans-Ecuadorian Pipeline (TEP) climbs from a thousand feet above sea level to 13,300 feet above sea level in the relatively short distance of 125 miles, making some cite the TEP as an example of the "technical feasibility" of a pipeline from Pakistan to China. However, further analysis causes that comparison to fall short, because at 310 miles the TEP is only about one-fifth the length of the proposed pipeline from Pakistan to China and does not cross territory rampant with insurgent activity and general instability.

Pipelines face substantial physical security risks. The oil from Pakistan would be required to be pumped through a remote terrain in potentially insecure areas where it would be more prone disruptions than the sea lanes. In case of any eventuality, oil tankers at sea can be rerouted, while pipelines are fixed links between the producer and consumer. It has been seen in the past that terrorists have carried out only a handful of successful attacks on oil tankers elsewhere in the world. However, non-state actors in Iraq and other countries have been able to successfully disrupt oil pipeline operations on a regular basis despite preventative action by security forces. Pipelines offer a wealth of targeting options to non-state actors. Destruction of an oil pipeline is a simple operation - an attacker only needs to know where the line is and use explosives to rupture it. Such disruptions would require immediate repairs in an area having hostile population which would require additional security measures. More critical vulnerabilities would include pump stations, storage facilities, pipeline terminals and the power supplies that run pumps and other key equipment. Though most of these facilities would be difficult for non - state actors to target successfully due to presence of security forces, targeting several thousand kilometres of unguarded pipeline would much easy. During an interstate conflict, the dynamics would be different. Modern military forces equipped with precision-guided munitions could easily target pumping stations and other vital points to disable pipelines carrying oil or gas into China.

China has been able to sustain its growth rate despite global recession. It is also firmly projecting that growth into the strategic domain. China-Pakistan nexus has been a major irritant in Sino - Indian ties. Notwithstanding of all drawbacks ie political, economic and security, Gwadar Port will provide China an outpost to monitor Indian naval movement in Persian Gulf and Arabian Sea. It will also provide an alternative to Pakistan Navy to survive in case of a blockade by India. The road and rail network from Kashgar to Gwadar port will route Chinese goods destined for the Middle East and other global destinations from Urumqi through Gwadar. The fibre optic link is likely to enhance China's cyber capability and will place India in a cyber-pincer.

Implications for India

China has always been interested that Pakistan continues to retain its control over POK. This not only ensures its own vital interests in Gwadar are protected but also it frustrates India's access to Central Asia. The proposed economic corridor would pass through the POK which implies that China has given a de facto acceptance of the Pakistan's claim on the disputed area. The Pak-China economic corridor has immense strategic implications for India. It will reduce India's option with regard to military action against Pakistan's blatant involvement in cross-border terrorism. Considering the strategic imperative of the corridor, China would be sensitive about its security. In fact, the economic corridor can be more appropriately referred to as a strategic corridor, which will make China a key player in the Persian Gulf. India is likely to be threatened with a two-front situation. The recent Chinese incursions in Ladakh need to be examined carefully. A muted response by India is likely to convey surrender of its claim on POK. Also, the Sino-Pak nexus will develop into a cohesive force against India in all international forums for India's fight to regain the disputed territory. India will have to formulate its response and policy on the assumption that the corridor will yield dividends as per the expectations of both China and Pakistan. India must register its strong protest against the project. It needs to take firm measures to secure her future ambitions. It needs to ensure that the boundary question with China does not get enlarged and it must be not allowed become a party to the Kashmir dispute.

6 | OPTIONS FOR INDIA TO COUNTER CHINA – PAKISTAN NEXUS

Increased Engagement with China

According to political observers, the global political architecture is undergoing a transformation with power increasingly shifting to the East, in what has been called the Asian Century. The two most populous nations on the earth, China and India, are on their way to becoming economic powerhouses and are shedding their reticence in asserting their global profiles, all of which makes their relationship of still greater importance for the international system. The future of this Asian Century will, to a large extent, depend upon the relationship between these two regional giants and the bilateral relationship between them will define the contours of the new international political architecture in Asia and the world at large.

The importance of their relationship has not been lost on either country. China and India have coordinated their efforts on wide-ranging issues. It is being contended that the forces of globalization have led to a certain convergence of Sino-Indian interests in the economic realm, as the two nations become even more deeply engaged in the international trading economy and more integrated in global financial networks. The attempt on the part of China in recent years has been to build its bilateral relationship with India on the basis of the larger world view of international politics on the part of both nations. As New Delhi and Beijing discovered a distinct convergence of their interests on the world stage, they have used it to strengthen their bilateral relations. They have established and maintained regular reciprocal high-level visits between political leaders. There has been a serious attempt to improve trade relations and China has sought to compartmentalize intractable issues with India that make it difficult for their bilateral relationship to move forward.

Chinese President Xi Jinping was one of the first foreign leaders to visit India soon after PM Modi came to power. It showed his keenness to strengthen India-China ties which have seen ups and downs. With the change in government, India has shown a new robustness in its dealings with China. New Delhi is signalling that there are limits to what is negotiable in Sino-Indian ties. In particular, it has adopted a harder line on Tibet by making it clear to Beijing that it expects China to reciprocate on Jammu and Kashmir, just as India has respected Chinese sensitivities on Tibet and Taiwan.

The four-day visit to China by India's External Affairs Minister followed by a visit by PM Modi reflects India's growing clout in the region. The Foreign Minister attended the Russia, India, China (RIC) foreign ministers' conference where they reached an understanding on fighting terrorism. China and Russia have agreed to support India for moving a proposal at the UN to punish those who shelter and finance terrorism essentially goes against Pakistan. This is a rare occasion when China, a close ally of Pakistan, has taken a stand on an issue that is likely to go against Pakistan. Beijing's move not only reflects the importance it accords to New Delhi, but is also an acknowledgment of its own problem of terrorism in Xinjiang province. China and Russia have also supported India's inclusion in the 21-member APEC and the Shanghai Cooperation Organisation. They also want India to play a greater role in the UN. India on its part should continue to engage China constructively especially on the issue of terrorism which will marginalise Pakistan considerably. If the Chinese trend continues then it is likely that Pakistan would also be induced to change its adversarial attitudes towards India.

Assertive Engagement with Pakistan

India needs to redefine its relations with Pakistan. It will have to indicate red lines which Pakistan cannot cross. India should not hold any peace parleys with Pakistan on issues that affect its national security. Till the time Pakistan does not change its belligerent attitude towards India, only trade and commerce, economic cooperation and people-to people exchanges should be allowed. Should Pakistan indulge in any misadventures against India, then India needs to retaliate appropriately not only by military action but also by applying pressure against Pakistan in Baluchistan, Sindh and the Northern Areas. Such actions by India will convey a stern message to Pakistan.

India's strategy for Pakistan must include diplomatic pressure, economic sanctions and military actions. The present government in India has signalled its intent by calling off the talks between the foreign ministers and retaliating with force to Pakistan's recent shelling across the border. Pakistan has its own vulnerabilities which are many times higher than India and in its strategic calculus it cannot ignore the threat that India can pose. Pakistan's future is a real wildcard. In a worst case scenario, internal violence and instability would even scare off its Chinese ally. In a best case, Islamabad would act to realize its own economic interests through normalized relations with India.

Renewed Indo – US Relations

USA's inaction on China's assistance to Pakistan's nuclear weapons and missiles programme has resulted in Pakistan becoming a rogue nuclear weapons state. China's growing military might and assertive behaviour has resulted in the manifestation of a joint nuclear and military threat to India's security and a wider threat to Indo Pacific stability and peace. Today, the differing US perceptions with India on China and Pakistan and its resultant effects on the security of the region has led United States and India to come together. One of the focuses of the recent visit of the American President to India was the growing might of China and the state sponsored terrorism by Pakistan. The United States is working to renew its relationship with India with the hopes that India's increasing economic and military strength could tip the power balance in Asia, as China continues to rise. The US has pledged to help India work toward becoming a global leader in a variety of ways: $4 billion in trade and investment and a new 10-year defence framework. India on its part wants to use the relationship with the United States to counter China, benefiting from the increased access to American technology. As far as Pakistan is concerned, India and USA have advanced their counter terrorism dialogue and recommitted to cooperating against Pakistan-based groups such as the Lashkar-e-Taiba (LeT).

This renewed relationship between USA and India has revealed India's strategic importance to American plans to counter an assertive China. The intimate US-India military relationship has generated fears of encirclement in China. India's position astride China's key maritime shipping lanes has made the prospect of a Washington-Delhi axis particularly worrisome. The United States and India both seek to spread democracy, expand trade and investment, counter terrorism, and, above all, keep the region peaceful by balancing China's growing military power. As Washington expands its presence in Asia as part of its rebalancing policy, India will become a critical partner. This relationship would be of advantage to India as it is likely to pose a caution to China and Pakistan from undertaking any misadventure against it.

CONCLUSION

Close Sino-Pak relations are nothing new for India. Looking into the future, China's expanding influence in Central Asia and its interest in overland access to the Arabian Sea could motivate even stronger links with Pakistan. The nexus is a live threat for India having military and non-military manifestations. These are irreversible strategic realities which India cannot ignore. India's foreign policy formulations and initiatives must factor in these threats and determine the course and direction of its foreign policy and response to threats emanating from the nexus. Irrespective of the rise of Chinese military prowess and the fact that it is arming Pakistan, India needs to develop suitable military capabilities without hurting the growing Indo China economic relations – a fact that gives immense leverage to both countries while the western economies are melting.

REFERENCES

1. An Alliance or Nexus against India: China-Pakistan Strategic Alliance and Kashmir Problem – Analysis by Asif Ahmed.

2. China-Pakistan Nuclear Alliance, IPCS Special Report, August 2011.

3. Evaluating a Rocky India-China-Pakistan relationship, Ramananda Sengupta Al Jazeera Centre for Studies.

4. CRS Report RL31555, China and Proliferation of Weapons of Mass Destruction and Missiles: Policy Issues.

5. China, India, and the "Whole Set-Up and Balance of the World"-Shashank Joshi.

6. China's New Foreign Policy "Assertiveness". Motivations and Implications - Suisheng Zhao.

7. China's 'String of Pearls' in Southern Asia-Indian Ocean: Implications for India and Taiwan -W.Lawrence S. Prabhakar.

8. China's Military Modernization: Responses from India – Arun Sahgal.

9. Deeper than the Indian Ocean? An Analysis of Pakistan--China Relations- SISA Report No.16 2014.

10. Indian Military's Cold Start Doctrine: Capabilities, Limitations and Possible Response from Pakistan- SASSI Research Paper 32.

11. India's strategic future: 2025 - Strategic Foresight Group, Mumbai, India.

12. Pakistan-China Relations: Where They Go From Here? UNISCI Discussion Papers.

13. Is Gwadar Port an Economic Haven for Balochistan and Pakistan? -Tousif Ali Yousaf.

14. China and Pakistan: Emerging Strains in the Entente Cordial- Isaac B.Kardon.

15. India – China in 2030: A Net Assessment of the Competition between Two Rising Powers- Mick Ryan.

16. ETIM's presence in Pakistan and China's growing pressure – Norwegian Peace Building Resource Centre – Aug 2014.

17. China and Pakistan: Fair-Weather Friends - Michael Beckley.

18. Crux of Asia – China, India and the Emerging Global Order – Carnegie Endowment.

19. The Pakistan Thorn in China-India-U.S Relations- Harsh V. Pant.

20. The China-Pakistan Alliance: Rhetoric and Limitations- Asia Programme Paper ASP PP 2012/01.

21. China Factor in India Pakistan Conflict-Asia Pacific Centre for Security Studies.

22. The Limits of the Pakistan–China Alliance -Lisa Curtis and Derek Scissors.

23. India's Foreign Policy 2012: A Critical Review in Relation to China and Pakistan Military Threats – Dr SubhashKapila.

24. Expansion of the Karakoram Corridor: Implications and Prospects –Senge H Sering.

25. The Red Shadow in Pakistan Occupied Kashmir: Aditi Malhotra.

26. India-China Relations – An Introspection: AmbSaurabh Kumar Sept 2014.

27. Nuclear Weapons Stability or Anarchy in the 21st Century:

China, India, and Pakistan-Thomas W. Graham, Ph.D. Brookhaven National Laboratory.

28.   India's Strategic Articulation: Shift in Thinking –IDSA Policy Brief.

29.   The growing Complexity in Sino – India Relations- Harish Pant.

30.   Pakistan in 2015-IPCS Special Report # 170 January 2015.

Index

Aircraft Rebuild Factory (ARF) 20

Nanchang A-5 and F-7 combat aircraft 20

Shenyang F-6, FT-5, FT-6 jet trainer aircraft 20

Pakistan Air Force 19, 31

A-5C Fantan FGA aircraft 19

F-7M Airguard fighter aircraft 19

F-7MG fighters 19

J-10/FC-20 FGA aircrafts, 19

k-8 trainer/combat aircrafts 19

Y-12 transport aircrafts 19

Pakistan Navy 21, 22, 23, 61

Hainan class submarine chasers 21

Hegn class fast attack missile craft 21

Huang Fen class fast attack missile craft 21

Huchuan class fast attack hydrofoil craft 21

Shanghai-II class fast patrol/gun boats 21

Mintaka Pass 57

Multi-Role Combat Aircraft 19

N

National Technical Research Organization 30

North Korea 16, 25, 28, 38

Nuclear Collaboration v

Nuclear Cooperation Agreement 36

Nuclear Non-Proliferation Treaty 37

Nuclear Suppliers Group 37, 39, 42, 44

O

Operation Parakram 7, 17

Osama bin Laden 10, 17, 20

P

Pakistan-China Oil Pipeline 59

Pakistan Remote Sensing Satellite 48

PAKSAT-1 46

PAKSAT-1R 46

People's Republic of China 1

Persian Gulf 52, 54, 60, 61, 62

Phalcon AWACS 29

PLA Air Force 21

PNS NASR 22

Port of Singapore Authority 54

Port Qasim 54

Pressler Amendment 22, 36

Q

Qing class submarines 22

R

Radar Maintenance Centre (RMC) 21

www.ingramcontent.com/pod-product-compliance
Lightning Source LLC
Chambersburg PA
CBHW021525270326
41930CB00008B/1095